Sew Up a Home Makeover

Sew Up a *Home Makeover*

50 Simple Sewing Projects to Transform Your Space

lexie barnes

Storey Publishing

For my boys: Henry, Sebastian, Monty, and Calvin,
and for my fella, Cory.
My home is wherever you are.

The mission of Storey Publishing is to serve our customers by
publishing practical information that encourages
personal independence in harmony with the environment.

Edited by Deborah Balmuth and Nancy D. Wood
Art direction and book design by Jessica Armstrong

Cover photography by © John Gruen, except for back cover, top left
 by Mars Vilaubi, and author photo by Claire Folger
Interior photography by © John Gruen, except for pages 12, 16, and 22 by © Lexie Barnes; 21,
 30, 34, 38–39, 76–77, 83 right, 88, 100–101, 107, 128–129, 145, and 149 left by Mars Vilaubi
Photo styling by Raina Kattelson
Illustrations by Christine Erikson
Decorative patterns by © iStockphoto.com/Ekaterina Romanova,
 except for pages 38–75 and 131–159 by © Lexie Barnes

Indexed by Nancy D. Wood

Storey Publishing
210 MASS MoCA Way
North Adams, MA 01247
www.storey.com

Printed in the United States by Versa Press
10 9 8 7 6 5 4 3 2 1

Library of Congress Cataloging-in-Publication Data

Barnes, Lexie.
 Sew up a home makeover / by Lexie Barnes.
   p. cm.
 Includes index.
 ISBN 978-1-60342-797-5 (pbk. : alk. paper)
 1. House furnishings. 2. Machine sewing.
 3. Textile fabrics in interior decoration. I. Title.
TT387.B383 2011
646.2'1—dc22
                        2010051178

ACKNOWLEDGMENTS

I am hugely indebted to the following fabulous people:

Deborah Balmuth, whose direction and leadership is inspiring; Amy Greeman, who makes me laugh and keeps me sane; Nancy D. Wood, without whom I'd never be able to say all that I want to say; Alethea Morrison, Jessica Armstrong, John Gruen, and Raina Kattelson, who make me — and my work — look so damn good; Pam Art, Dan Reynolds, and the Storey family for their continued support, patience, and partnership with me on this project.

The wonderful team at Peter Fasano, especially Janie Goldenberg and Peter for their time, help, and use of the gorgeous Peter Fasano fabrics. (And for letting Calvin explore your supercool studio while we talked shop!)

The kind (and quick!) folks at Spoonflower for making magic happen in the eleventh hour; the sweet and generous Caroline of jcarolinehome! and jcaroline-creative!; the stellar staff at Purl Soho (both coasts); the fab gals at Bolt in Fabric Boutique in Portland, Oregon, and Charlie and Lindsey of Hawthorne Thread. At home in Massachusetts: Bill Muller and Ali Osborn of Guild Art Center and Liz Karney of Sticks and Bricks for contributing her time and talent to make our ginormous headboard.

Everyone who works for and with the lexie barnes studio: Amy Hill, Maggie Couture, Kristen Valle, Peter Irvine, Amy Wright, Joanna Roche, Will Brideau, Chris Gondek, Ali Puffer, Megan Zinn, and all of the gifted vendors who participate in Twist, our funky little craft show in Northampton.

Our fabulous sewing crew: Beth Boggia, Caitlin Bosco, Alexis Cormier, Jeri Duncan, Margot Glass, Shahan Rose Hart, Roxanne Morris, Jen Moulton, Anne Persand, and Sarah Platanitis. Thank you, ladies! You are amazing and I am so grateful to have had the pleasure of working with such a talented bunch.

Everyone who volunteered to help out and waited so patiently: Andrea Combes, Rita Goldberg, Adina Klein, Sarah Michna, Megan Risley, Ryan Rogers, Robbin Skinner, and Tanya Thomann.

My dear friends Gina Giangrosso, Naira Francis, and Jeanette Malone just for being there, always being there; Claire Folger and Claudia Moriel for their years of encouragement and generosity; Laura Kroll for pitching in; Shoshana Phillips of Red Horse Press and Deborah Goldstein of Miss Wit Designs for their diversions and inspiration; Betsy Strickland of Farmhouse Wares and Kim Lambert for their wisdom and friendship.

My family: Patti Barnes, Cheryl Carson, Irene Hill, Ben Klaff and Emily Hermant, Ramsay and Gary Klaff, Adam Scheffler, and Linda and Philip Scheffler.

More than anything, I wish to thank with all my heart my husband, Cory, and our sons, Henry, Sebastian, Monty, and Calvin, for letting me take over every conceivable surface in the house for way too long; for letting me work when I should have been playing; and for being there at the end of the day, no matter what, with open arms. I love you forever.

Contents

Introduction

THIS ISN'T A BOOK ABOUT DECORATING, and it isn't really a book about sewing, either. This is a book about little changes that make a big difference. Creating a home of any size, at any stage of life, is exciting. Finding the time and resources to make it just the way you want may seem, at best, overwhelming, and at worst, impossible. After you've been in your home for a period of time, it might start to feel too familiar, or dated, or (gulp) boring. This book is full of projects you can make and ideas you can use to add refreshing elements to your living spaces — without breaking the bank or making your family, friends, or yourself crazy in the process! Everything in here is easy to make, without complicated patterns or templates to follow. You can easily customize the projects to suit your style, taste, needs, and budget.

In my house, there's always some kind of makeover happening. We move the furniture around, we paint, we refinish, we build, and we sew. All of the makeovers are satisfying, but using fabric for your home makeover projects is particularly rewarding because you can really see the bigger transformations happening as each little project comes to life.

Don't worry about giving the entire house or apartment a makeover all at once. And don't think you have to move to a new place every time a room feels a little stale. You already have what it takes to make the changes you'd like to see at home: imagination, ingenuity, common sense, and enthusiasm. You don't have to start at the beginning of the book and make every project in order. You just have to get started. Skip around and see what inspires you. Then hop to it! It's time for your makeover!

~ lexie

CHAPTER 1

Makeover Magic

THE SIX BASIC PRINCIPLES OUTLINED IN THIS CHAPTER can help you assess, map out, and achieve your decorating goals — and have a lot of fun while you're doing it! These principles are the same, no matter who you are or where you live. First, you'll figure out the style you're going for. Next, think about how each room or piece needs to function, as well as how to keep it comfortable for you, your cohabitants, and your guests. Take stock of what you already own, what you should get rid of, and what you need to find, make, or buy. Then, look realistically at your budget and your time. Once you've considered these six points, you'll be ready to take on everything, going room by room, one makeover project at a time, until your home is exactly the way you want it to be.

Style

The first step to decorating, we're often told, is to "define your style." This is much easier said than done for most people. I, for one, have never been able to do it. I am fickle and curious and always looking for new ways to express myself through my work, my wardrobe, and my home décor. If I'm feeling "urban romantic" one day, "retro chic" a week later, and "modern bohemian" the day after that, what label should I assign to myself — and to my home?

If you're like me, and constantly changing your mind, you can't really label yourself at all, can you? If you changed your décor as often as you change your mood, it would be a very confusing — and expensive — way to live. It's easy to trade out last year's boots for this season's hottest new jeans, but what about your living space? Wallpaper stays up there, right? And you can't just pull up carpeting because it doesn't go with your dress. To decorate your home means you have to commit, don't you? Not exactly.

FIRST, remember that a successfully decorated room is really a collection of individual elements that come together. It's not a fixed and permanent definition of "who you are." Just like you, your home will grow and develop with time. It's surprisingly easy to make little changes now, allowing you to express the different facets of your personality, while maintaining a successful overall tone or vibe to your home. If you change one or two of those smaller elements, the whole room can look and feel a little different. So when you are feeling flirtatious or bored, you don't have to move or overhaul the whole house! Just throw on a coat of paint, blend in some new pieces, or move things around and watch the transformation begin.

SECOND, no one expects you to furnish and decorate your entire house overnight. Sure, we think that's how it should happen. We imagine that everyone else's home is completely "done" before they turn the key and that we're the only ones standing in an empty room without a clue how to begin. But

Good morning, sunshine! Brighten up the breakfast table with sweet handmade table linens (see page 79).

the reality, even for folks with a big budget and a lot of help from professional decorators, is that it takes time to build a nest that feels like home. You can — and should — let your style evolve. Take the time to figure out what you like and what you don't like. Start with one thing you love and build from there. Maybe it's a piano, a painting, or your couch. Maybe it's the color blue or a pillow you made. Trust your gut and your own taste, and let your look grow.

Function

It's been said that "form follows function," and it's true. You need to consider how a space will be used before you decorate it. For instance, think of your ideal kitchen — not what it looks like, but what you do in it. Are you grabbing a snack from the cupboard and running out the door? Just passing through? Or will you be cooking regular family dinners or hosting parties? Maybe you like to work in your kitchen. Will you need a desk or tabletop dedicated to something other than typical kitchen activities?

In our kitchen, we wanted a "kid station" with ample storage for art and craft supplies, workbooks, reference books, and learning materials, plus enough room for all four of my kids to work on projects and homework. This was important to us, so we planned our kitchen knowing that part of it would be reserved for these activities. Knowing how we wanted it to function helped us determine the layout, lighting, colors, and furniture. It also helped us organize the other part of the kitchen, where we prepare and eat our meals. Everyone's needs are different. Someone else could move into the same house and turn our creativity center into a baking station instead. The point is to think about how you will use each space and then plan accordingly.

Do this for every room in the house. Do you like to read in your bedroom? That might require a comfy chair and a good reading lamp. Would you prefer to keep your exercise equipment there, so you can jump out of bed and onto your elliptical first thing in the morning? Once you've assessed your needs and mapped out the rooms functionally, you can start infusing your style and personality throughout the house.

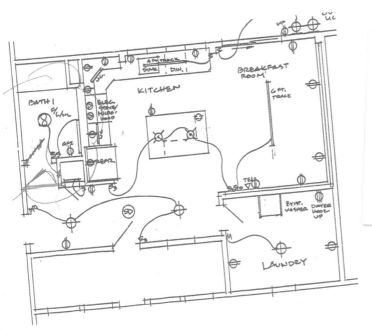

The plan made real!

The design plan for our kitchen included a "kid station" to accommodate the activities of our four busy kids in the midst of all the other kitchen happenings.

INSPIRATION

Even if you already know your likes and dislikes, it's a good idea to start looking for inspiration. Start a collection of images and notes about rooms, colors, patterns, palettes, textures, and furniture. You can use a binder, a folder, or a shoebox, or you might prefer to scan the images and start a virtual scrapbook. It doesn't matter how you store them, just start collecting ideas.

One of my favorite techniques is what I call the "flip and rip." Flip quickly through magazines and rip out the pictures that catch your eye immediately. These are the things that attract you right away, so you will definitely want those in your collection. Over time, you'll see that you are drawn to the same look or feeling again and again. You can define it by giving it any name you like, or you don't have to name it at all. You'll simply start to recognize your taste and watch your style define itself. Be sure to sift through the file from time to time and weed out any images that no longer strike you or you've outgrown. You want this collection to reflect what you love most; what you leave out is just as important as what you put in.

Comfort

When we talk to friends about our childhood homes, we don't typically start off by telling them about how well the living room was laid out for entertaining. When we think of home, we think first of comfort. A good floor plan helps, of course, but what we're talking about here are the things inside our home that make us feel cozy. Sure, we know about sofas, beds, linens, napkins, and rugs. These are soothing, comforting objects that help us associate home with our personal sense of security.

Beyond the soft furnishings, we also can consider colors, textures, and building materials. Imported tiles might be gorgeous on the kitchen floor but pretty hard on a toddler who's just learning to get around. Carpeting is very comfortable unless you happen to have dust mite allergies, in which case, hardwood floors might be better. Dining room chairs should have enough cushioning and back support for you and your guests to enjoy sitting down together. A great-looking chair makes a nice statement, but an aching back after a dinner party is pretty memorable, too.

Comfort is an important factor often misunderstood, overlooked, or traded in for style. Think carefully about comfort and what it means to you. Then, look for ways to incorporate comfort into your home.

Top: Loud and proud! Mix bold, strong patterns in first one or two colors to maximize the wow factor. Add a surprising texture, like the fluffy faux bear rug, to keep it fun and unexpected.

Bottom: Day for night. Neutral colors keep the bedroom calm and tranquil, but a splash of color on the duvet underside adds morning cheer.

Inventory

Chances are, you already have a lot of stuff: furniture, appliances, knickknacks, and soft furnishings, such as rugs, curtains, sheets, and so on. Now is the time to go through the house room by room and figure out what stays and what needs to go. It's almost never necessary to toss everything out and start from scratch, even if you secretly wish you could do a big overnight overhaul. Usually, you can do a lot with what you already have. Some small creative changes can make a really big difference.

Can any furniture items or accessories be moved from one room to another, where they might serve you better? Can anything be modified for a new purpose? Try using what you have first, before heading out to shop. Think about why you want to make changes and then figure out how to reach those goals.

On the flip side, don't hang on to stuff that doesn't work just because you already own it. It might be time to graduate from the flimsy futon of your college days to a new couch, even if "new" is still secondhand.

Quite often, we love and can still use what we have, but we just need to look at it in a new way. Maybe your Great Aunt Sue gave you a funky, old eggbeater that really doesn't work anymore. If it doesn't work in the room, it doesn't belong there. It's just a piece of junk now, taking up space in your drawer. If you really love it because it's as cool as Great Aunt Sue herself, then why not hang it on the wall instead? Or put it in a shadow box frame or on a shelf to display it as part of your personal history. Make that beater part of your décor. If it is a part of who you are, it just doesn't belong in a drawer with other tools you actually need to use. You could even build on it to create an eclectic, vintage look.

Budget

You might not need a formal budget, but it's a good idea to at least make a prioritized list. Big-ticket items are called such because they are expensive, and the collective cost of little things can really add up. When deciding how to spend for your home, it's best to pay attention to the details. Look at projects individually, as well as how each one affects the overall budget you have.

If you're planning to tackle smaller projects on a regular basis, you can create a monthly budget, allocating a little bit of cash toward buying fabric or paint. If you need to work on entire rooms, you might want to give yourself an annual spending budget for home improvement. If you are buying a new place, you should absolutely consider the cost of renovations, improvements, and decorating, and incorporate those costs into your home-buying budget. A little bit of planning goes a long way, and although it takes extra effort, you'll be happy — and relieved — when you see you are spending and saving wisely.

Timeline

Now that you've identified your decorating needs, sussed out your style, and balanced your budget, you have to figure out how and when to make it all happen. Some people are great planners and like to stick to a schedule. And then there are those who jump in and start stripping off the wallpaper in every room without a clue of what they'll put up next — or what's behind the paper they're so keen to tear down!

One approach is to do one room at a time, but with our busy schedules and limited budgets, it's really difficult for most of us to finish a whole room before moving on to another one. Try taking on one project at a time. Whether it's something small, like making a potholder, or a bigger task, like painting the halls, try to choose a project, plan it out carefully, and get it done. You can move on to the next one right away, but get that first one completely out of the way before getting started. You'll enjoy the satisfaction of working in smaller chunks and watching your home start to come together as you go along.

PREPPING TO PAINT

Paired with bright white trim and a lot of sunshine, these dramatic steel gray walls bring sophistication to a simple bedroom in a farmhouse.

PAINTING COMPLETE!

CHAPTER 2

Fabrics and Tools

WHETHER YOU ARE A SEWING NOVICE OR AN EXPERIENCED SEAMSTRESS, just knowing more about the process will allow you to enjoy it a whole lot more. First, you need to get familiar with fabric. Trust me, when you're standing in a giant warehouse full of "options," you'll be glad you looked over a primer before you got there. Next, say hello to the handy tools you'll meet along the way. Understanding what they're for helps you select the right ones for the job. Once you start building your own bag of tricks, making bigger decisions will be a snap.

Fabrics

When selecting fabrics for your projects, you'll need to consider where the finished piece will go. Will it need to be machine washable? Will it be in direct sunlight or get a lot of wear? Will your pets lie on it? For homemade projects, you can use lightweight fabrics to make smaller items that require interfacing or for machine-washable items like napkins and dish towels. Medium-weight fabrics are great for seat coverings, tote bags, and some window treatments. Use heavier fabrics for dramatic effect — drapes or luxurious pillows made from velvet can make quite an impact. Upholstery fabric is just what you need for projects like the headboard, bench, and room screen.

When in doubt, ask the staff at your local fabric store. Most folks who work in a fabric store have a lot of experience with the stuff, and you'll be surprised at how much helpful information they are willing to share with you.

GOOD TO KNOW

All projects can be made from 44/45"-wide fabric unless otherwise noted. Most home décor weight fabrics are wider, which will give you yardage left over for other spontaneous ideas.

FIRST THINGS FIRST

It's a good idea to look at fabrics first when decorating. It's much easier to match a paint color to a sofa or shower curtain than to do it the other way around. When you are making your own soft furnishings, you have the luxury of choosing from a wider variety of fabrics. Take the time to look for fabrics you love. You can mix and match colors, patterns, and textures any way you like. Don't be afraid to try things out! Feel the fabrics, ask questions, and do a little homework if you need to. Sometimes it takes a little trial and error, but as you get more practice, you'll figure out what works for you and your home.

Start building a collection of your favorite fabrics to keep on hand when inspiration strikes!

A Look at Fabric Types

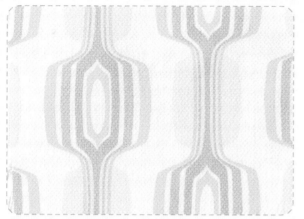

CANVAS. The fabric is made from a variety of sources, including cotton, linen, jute, or hemp. The term is also used to indicate any heavy, tightly woven fabric. It's strong and sturdy, and available in a wide variety of colors, prints, and weights. It's a good choice for projects like the Butterfly Chair Cover (see page 57), when you want something durable and strong.

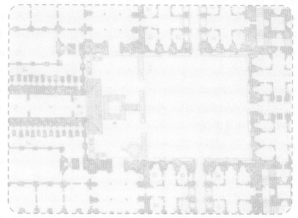

COTTON. Made from a natural fiber derived from the cotton plant, cotton fabric is available in a wide range of weights and textures. Basic quilting fabrics are usually 100 percent cotton and that's what you'll find on bolts at your local quilting or fabric shop. There are countless colors and prints from which to choose and you'll fall in love just browsing through them.

DENIM. This cotton fabric is most commonly used for blue jeans. Sturdy and pliable, it is easily laundered and can really take a beating. Denim is now available in many colors and some prints as well. It would be a good choice for the Flirty Floor Mat (see page 44).

FLANNEL. A light- to medium-weight fabric, flannel is typically made from cotton, a cotton blend, or wool. Very soft and warm, flannel is best known for use in bedsheets, nightgowns, and plaid shirts. Fine for use on its own, flannel also makes a nice lining. You can use it instead of fleece to line the Tea Cozy (see page 82).

FLEECE. This soft, lightweight fabric is made from polyester or recycled plastic bottles (PET). It is available in a variety of weights, piles, and textures. Because fleece is easy to care for, insulating, and breathable, it is an excellent choice for projects like our Improv Appliqué Blankie (see page 109).

LINEN. A natural fiber derived from flax, linen is a strong, lightweight fabric available in many wonderful colors. While its beauty will dazzle you, it does have some drawbacks. It tends to wrinkle, though you can usually hand- or machine-wash it, and you'll have to iron it well. It can be pricey. That said, linen is a lovely way to dress up any room. We used linen to make the Roman Shade (see page 67) and Bolster Pillows (see page 70).

MUSLIN. When you are trying something new, you might consider a "first draft" made out of inexpensive muslin. It will save you money, not to mention grief over the loss of a beloved vintage remnant you've been waiting to use!

VELVET. A tufted, woven fiber with a thick, soft pile, velvet is considered luxurious and is often associated with royalty. Velvet can make simple home projects like curtains and pillow covers feel fancy and elegant.

How Much to Buy

I always recommend talking to your local fabric store. Tell them what you are planning to make and how big you want it to be, and they can help you buy enough fabric. Bring in your sketch or measurements and show it to them. I always tend to buy more than I need, just in case. I like to have leftover scraps to use for trim or matching accents, or for another project.

NOTE: *You should allow extra yardage for directional prints, when you'll need the motifs to be right side up, or when you'll need to line up the designs across the project.*

Color

Color has a huge impact on how we feel and think. Warm colors — reds, oranges, yellows, and gold — are cozier and can make rooms feel smaller. Cool colors — greens, blues, and violets — create a lighter, more open feeling. The lighting, both natural and artificial, will change the effects of any color you choose, so be sure to test the way a color looks in different light and at different times of day. You can choose a single palette for your entire home or treat each room as a discrete space with its very own palette. Create an idea board and start by pinning fabric swatches to it. You can add wallpaper samples and paint chips to it to see how everything goes together.

Fabric Jargon

SELVAGE. This is the finished edge on either side of the fabric. Selvages are designed to keep the fabric from unraveling. Some are white with information printed about the fabric designer, some have little holes where the fabric was attached to the loom, some have fringy edges, and some are just plain.

GRAINLINE. The grainline of the fabric refers to the threads running parallel to the selvage. Sometimes this is called the straight (grain) of the fabric. The crosswise grain runs from selvage to selvage. You generally want to cut out the pieces for your projects along the grainline.

BIAS. The bias grain runs at a 45-degree angle to the selvage. When you pull fabric along the bias grain, you will notice that it stretches more in that direction than when you pull on the straight grain. Binding tape is cut along the bias, as stretchiness helps when stitching the tape around corners and curves.

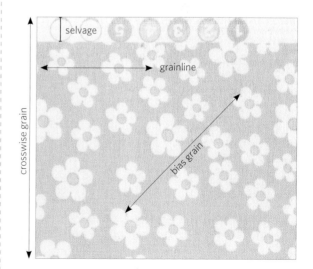

REARRANGE. REPURPOSE. REPAIR.

Don't think you have to run out and spend a fortune to give your home some makeovers. Take stock of what you already have. Flat sheets can become a duvet cover, a shower curtain can be turned into porch pillows, and dish towels make a cleverly converted set of curtains. If you can't afford a new bed, why not make a headboard instead?

You can also move things around when working on your makeovers. Swap the lamps from the living room with the ones in the bedroom. Slipcover some folding chairs from the basement and your dining room will look brand new. You can convert a bench into a coffee table, a dresser into a bedside table, and even a closet into a playroom. Some elbow grease and a little ingenuity will save you money and time — and inspire you to keep thinking out of the box. The turn of a screw, a fresh coat of paint, a few clever stitches, and your imagination might be all you need to make over your home.

A) Tired dresser drawers . . .

B) Dressed for success!

C) A dingy, dated telephone table . . .

D) Revived and updated for a happy hallway.

Notions and Tools

Here's the stuff you need to get started. The basic tools are easy to find at your local fabric store. You can order online, but be sure to ask any questions you have at the store and check the return policies before you make your purchase. There are a few things you don't want to skimp on, like needles, shears, and of course, your sewing machine. If you find a deal that looks too good to be true, it very well may be. Talk to the shop clerk or owner and get the skinny. Buyer beware = sewer prepared!

Your Sewing Machine

We assume that you have a basic sewing machine and know how to use it. With so many different sewing machines out there, we can't give specific instructions on how to operate yours. Refer to your manual if you need to. If you don't have a manual, you can find one online (see Resources) or invite a friend or family member to help get you started. The rest is just practice.

Once you can thread your machine and fill the bobbin, use scrap fabric to practice some stitching. Only two of the projects in this book require zippers, and for those you'll need a zipper foot. If you want to add buttons to anything you are making, your machine may have a buttonhole attachment. Get familiar with your machine, your manual, and how all of your attachments work.

MISSING MANUAL?

If you've inherited or bought a secondhand sewing machine that doesn't have a manual, all is not lost. You can often locate and order a manual for your machine online. Just do a search for the brand name of your machine.

A simple table, comfortable seat, and good lighting transform an empty corner into a terrific sewing station.

YOUR SEWING KIT

In addition to your sewing machine, you will want to have the following items on hand:

- Good, sharp shears used only for cutting fabric
- Good-quality pinking shears (which make a zigzag edge) to finish seams
- Rotary cutter, mat, and cutting ruler for long straight lines
- Small scissors for clipping and trimming
- Straight pins and a pincushion
- Magnet (a great tool for picking up spilled pins)
- Tape measure, sewing ruler, or yardstick; possibly also a seam gauge
- Variety of hand-sewing needles
- Variety of sewing machine needles
- Seam ripper
- Safety pin
- Dressmaker's chalk or disappearing fabric markers
- Steam iron and ironing board
- Point turner (see Shortcuts on page 26)
- Weights: paperweights, cans, or any small items with some heft, to hold down pieces of fabric while you are pinning and cutting
- Scrap paper of different weights, and pencil and eraser (for making templates)

Pins

Long straight pins with very big heads and very slender shafts are the best for most fabrics. Pins with glass heads are easier to see. Sturdier, longer upholstery pins are best for home décor and upholstery weight fabrics. A good pincushion or two makes it easy to grab a pin when you need one — or try a magnetic pin holder.

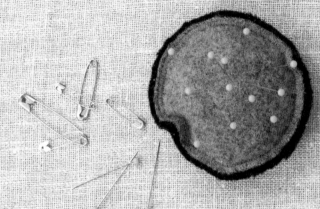

Needles

Sewing machine needles can get dull after only a few hours, so check them regularly for burrs and dull points, and always have spares available. Smaller needles are better for lightweight fabrics and larger needles should be used on heavier upholstery fabrics, as well as canvas, or denim. There are also specialty needles for some materials, like leather. You can check your sewing machine manual for guidance on how to choose the right needles or you can ask your neighborhood fabric shop.

Fabric Markers

When marking your measurements or template on the wrong side of a fabric, it's best to use water-soluble, nonpermanent marking pens. Test the pens on scraps of the fabric you're using, though, to make sure they don't stain, bleed, or show through to the other side. Another option is tailor's chalk, which comes in little squares or pencil form.

Thread

Thread comes in a variety of weights and types. Typically, you want to match the fiber content of your thread to that of the fabric you are working with. When it comes to colors, you can make your own choices. You can match the thread to the main color of the fabric or you might want to match it to one of the accent colors for impact. Using a contrasting color thread is a fun way to add oomph to a solid color fabric.

Shears or Scissors?

Technically, you call them scissors when the length is 6" or less and the finger holes are the same size. Shears are usually 7" to 12" long, with one larger finger hole (to fit two or more fingers). Whether you are using scissors or shears, it is important that they are comfortable and fit your hand. You'll want something that feels good to you, is easy to open and close, and isn't too heavy. There are even shears made for lefties! To keep fabric shears sharp, do not use them to cut paper, cardboard, aluminum foil, or hair!

Rotary Cutters and Mats

A rotary cutter and mat are excellent tools for all your sewing projects. They allow for speedy, tidy cutting and a perfectly straight line every time. But it's important to use them carefully. A rotary cutter is a very sharp tool with a round blade that is used to cut fabrics. It should only be used with a mat to protect surfaces underneath from being damaged. I also recommend using nonslip rulers that are specifically made for use with your rotary cutter and mat. Protect your precious fingers or you'll have to take a long break from your fun projects!

SHORTCUTS

• Although building a collection of cutting tools is helpful in the long run, you can actually get by with one pair of shears (a.k.a. scissors), as long as they are very sharp and cut all the way to the points.

• I use a tape measure for anything I'm measuring. I don't own a ruler or a yardstick. An important exception to this is when you're using a rotary cutter. You really need to use the cutter with a mat underneath, and a ruler designed for the task.

• A chopstick makes an excellent point turner (for pushing out corners when turning a stitched bag or pillow right side out). You can also use the eraser end of a pencil. But I don't recommend a pointed knitting needle; it could poke holes — yikes!

• If your iron doesn't have a steamer function, you can use a spray bottle and mist your fabric while pressing.

Interfacing

Interfacing is a layer of special fabric you can affix to the wrong side of your fabric for extra support and structure. It comes in a variety of weights and in two styles: fusible (iron-on) or sew-in. Some types for crafts and home décor come with a fusible surface on both sides. The projects in this book that require interfacing call for the fusible kind. Just make sure the sticky side is facing the fabric, or you'll get adhesive all over your iron.

Batting

Batting is cotton or man-made material used for filling, padding, or quilting. Batting is available in a variety of weights (or "lofts") and materials. You can use cotton, polyester, cotton-poly blends, or wool. If you aren't sure which type or loft you'll need, ask your local fabric or quilting store for guidance.

Staple Guns

A staple gun is used to drive or shoot staples, and is called for when attaching fabric to wood, as with the Reupholstered Seat (see page 42), the Upholstered Headboard (see page 64), or the Roman Shade (see page 67). Staple guns come in different sizes and types, ranging from light use to heavy duty. If you are lucky enough to own or have access to an electric staple gun, we recommend using one for the projects in this book. But a manual staple gun will also do the trick.

Staples come in different lengths, so check the size before you buy them. There are no hard-and-fast rules about what weight and length to use, but the most common staple used for upholstering is a 22-gauge staple, which comes in lengths of $\frac{5}{16}$", $\frac{7}{16}$", $\frac{1}{2}$", and $\frac{5}{8}$".

Seam Ripper

This small tool is used to unpick stitches without cutting into fabric. Great for opening seams, cutting off buttons, and taking out basting stitches, it's a "must have" tool!

Adhesives

When using adhesives, be sure to protect your work area. Scraps of cardboard or pieces of aluminum foil make terrific shields against droplets and overspray. With spray adhesives, it's best to spray outdoors. If you must spray inside, use adequate ventilation and protect the surrounding area with poster board or aluminum foil so everything around you doesn't get sticky!

HOT GLUE GUN AND GLUE STICKS. This hand-held, electrical tool holds a solid stick of glue. Solid cylinder sticks of glue are inserted into one end of the gun and are heated and melted when you squeeze the trigger. Glue guns are very easy to use and virtually indispensable for all kinds of craft, décor, and home improvement projects. There are a wide variety of styles, sizes, temperatures, and prices, ranging from a few dollars (for a small, kid-friendly, low-temp gun) to much larger, hotter, and pricier industrial models.

SPRAY ADHESIVE. Liquid glue under pressure in a can, this glue is applied as an aerosol spray. When the valve is pressed open, the adhesive is released as a mist. Spray adhesive has many properties, so when choosing, consider how quickly it dries and how tacky it is (from low-tack to extra-strong). There are spray adhesives made especially for fabric use and others that are multipurpose. Be sure to read instructions and warning labels carefully, as spray adhesive has toxic fumes.

FABRIC GLUE. These adhesives are specifically designed for use with fabric. Some bond permanently and are washable, making them ideal for bonding two fabrics together. Others are neither permanent nor washable, and are better suited for embellishment or decorative gluing. Fabric glue in spray form is excellent because it is low-tack and items can be repositioned easily. Read labels carefully or ask a salesperson for help making the best choice for the project at hand.

> ### SAFETY FIRST!
> - The melted glue in glue guns is extremely hot! Use caution when handling to prevent accidental burns.
> - Only use spray adhesive in a well-ventilated area or outdoors. Do not use around children or pets. For additional protection from fumes, you might want to use safety glasses and a mask, both available at hardware, big box, and craft stores.

CHAPTER 3

Tips and Techniques

MAYBE YOU LOVE THE IDEA OF A MAKEOVER, but you haven't the foggiest idea where to begin. Or maybe you have a gazillion ideas and worry that you don't know enough "tricks of the trade." Don't panic! Learning to sew — or getting better at it — takes practice. And your personal approach to sewing is just like your decorating style — unique. You can study the following techniques ahead of time, or refer back to this chapter as you need them. How you learn is totally up to you. You really only need a few basic skills and terms to make it through a sewing project, so even if you've never tried a makeover, I promise you — you can do it!

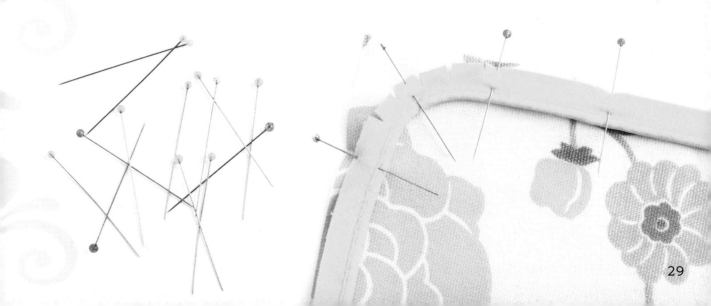

Basic Stitches

Most sewing machines have the same basic stitch settings, which can be changed or adjusted by turning a dial, for instance: stitch length, stitch width, and stitch tension. Be sure to read the section in your manual on how to make these adjustments. Here's a quick review of stitches and what they're good for:

NORMAL STITCH. This stitch is used for most seams. The normal stitch setting is 10–12 stitches per inch (2mm–2.5mm on metric machines).

BASTING STITCH. At 6–8 stitches per inch (3mm –4mm), this is the longest stitch on your sewing machine. Basting stitches are considered temporary and are easily removed. You can also do your basting stitches by hand.

SATIN STITCH. This refers to a set of stitches laid very closely side by side. We use it to finish a raw edge. It can be created with a zigzag setting (see below) and a tight setting for the number of stitches per inch.

ZIGZAG STITCH. This is used to stitch seams, finish raw edges, and for decoration. The manual (or a friend) will show you how to control, not only how many zigzag stitches per inch, but also the width of the stitch. It's a good idea to test different combinations to get a feel for what the stitch will look like on your fabric. You may need a separate zigzag presser foot with a wider needle opening when using this stitch.

THE MAGIC NUMBERS

It's a good idea to test your stitch length and tension when starting a new project. An easy way to perform the test is to take two scraps of the fabric you'll be using and sew them together. Check (and adjust as needed) the top thread and the bobbin thread of the stitching to make sure the tension and stitch length work well for that fabric and thread. When the stitches meet in the middle of the fabrics (not floating on the top or bottom), pin a piece of paper to the scrap and label it with the stitch length and/or width, tension, and kind of thread that you used. This will help when you are making more than one project at a time or have to leave the project and come back to it later.

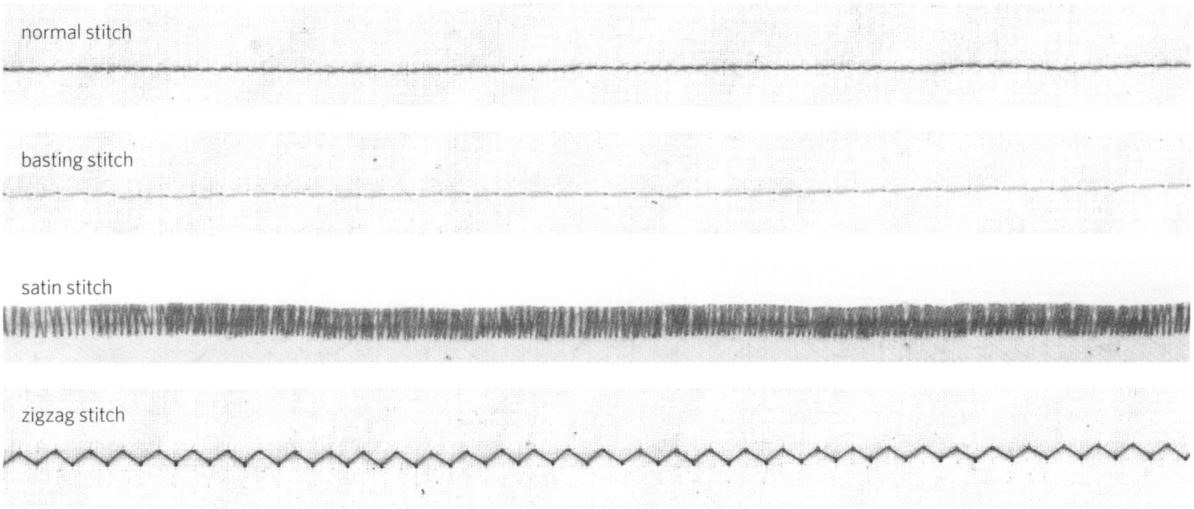

normal stitch

basting stitch

satin stitch

zigzag stitch

More Stitch Jargon

The following machine stitches are not settings on a dial. They describe how the stitching is used for a particular purpose. In most cases, a normal stitch setting is used.

BACKSTITCH. This term (also called *backtack*) refers to backing up and stitching in the opposite direction. Backstitching is used mostly at the beginning and end of a line of stitching to prevent it from coming undone. You don't backstitch on basting stitches, however, as they will be pulled out later.

EDGESTITCH. This refers to stitching close to the edge of a fabric piece, on the top of the right side. Edgestitching is done for reinforcement, decoration, or to hold an edge in place.

STAYSTITCH. This is a line of stitches sewn in the seam allowance ⅛" away from or almost on the seamline. This stitch is especially helpful on curves, to prevent stretching and/or prevent clipping too far into the seam allowance (see page 33).

TOPSTITCH. This means that the stitching shows on the "top" or the right side of the fabric. This stitch is usually decorative and sewn in one or more straight parallel lines about ¼" from the fabric edge.

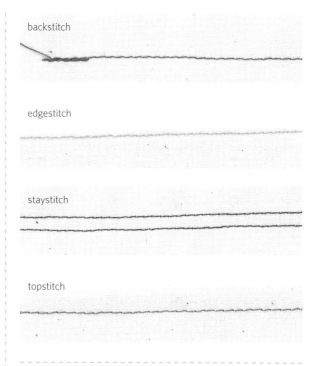

backstitch

edgestitch

staystitch

topstitch

THE BOX STITCH

A box stitch is made by stitching a square or rectangular box, and then stitching an X inside the box from corner to corner. This stitch is used to secure bag handles and is especially useful on larger bags, which will need extra reinforcement for strength.

1 (start here)

STITCHING BY HAND

Slipstitch is a nearly invisible finishing stitch (sometimes called a *blind stitch* or *blind hem*) that can be used to hem or to close an opening from the outside, as in the Bolster Pillows (see page 70) and other projects in this book. Slide the threaded needle between the two folded edges for about ½" (or one folded edge and a flat fabric, as with appliqué) so the knot will be hidden between the pieces of fabric. Pick up just a couple of threads to make your stitches and repeat them until finished.

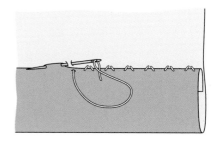

Seams and Hems

In a nutshell, seams are what you use to put your projects together and hems are how you finish the edges. There are many ways to sew both, each with a different purpose and look. Test them out on some practice fabric to see which ones you are most comfortable with. Every sewer has his or her favorite techniques and you'll find yours in no time!

Sew It Seams

Sewing seams is simple, and basic to the act of sewing. Here's how it's done:

1 Pin two pieces of fabric with right sides together.

   NOTE: *Your pins should be inserted perpendicular to the seam or edge. Position the pin heads to the right so you can easily remove them as you are stitching. You can space the pins as needed; I suggest starting at about 2" apart.*

2 Stitch the side you want to sew, ½" from the edge of the fabric. Remove the pins as you go, just before you stitch over them (otherwise, you might break the sewing machine needle).

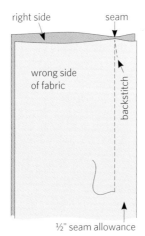

right side   seam

wrong side of fabric

backstitch

½" seam allowance

SEWING 101

* **SEAM.** *A line of stitching that joins two pieces of fabric.*

* **SEAM ALLOWANCE.** *The area between the raw edge of the fabric and the line of stitching.*

* **HEM.** *A common method of finishing a raw edge by turning it under once or twice and stitching.*

3 Backstitch at the beginning and end of the seam.

4 Trim the threads at the ends of the seam and remove any remaining pins.

5 On the wrong side of the fabric, open up the seam allowances and press the seam flat. In some cases, directions might call for pressing both seam allowances to one side.

Cutting Curves and Corners

For many of the simpler projects, you will essentially stitch squares of fabric together and turn them right side out. If you are not finishing the seams, you should at least trim them to a narrower, neater width, to prevent bulkiness. The corners, especially, need special attention. Clip the fabric diagonally across the corners to get rid of extra material that will get in the way of turning a neat corner.

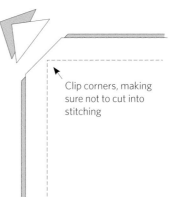

Clip corners, making sure not to cut into stitching

Several projects, such as the Bolster Pillows (see page 70) and the Wristlet Pouch (see page 141) require a curved seam. Concave seams (with an inward curve) are less bunchy when the curves are clipped. Convex seams (with an outward curve) need to be notched for the curve to lie flat. In either case, press the seam afterward for best results.

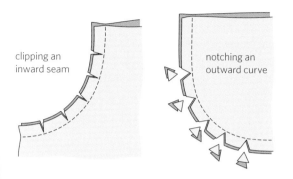

clipping an inward seam

notching an outward curve

Finishing Raw Edges

Along the outer edge of any seam allowance is a raw edge of fabric. This edge will not show, because it'll be on the inside of your project. But it's possible that the edge could fray or unravel with use or over time.

You'll see this for yourself when you prewash the fabric! Some fabrics fray very little, but others unravel quite a bit and you'll end up with a big mess. Whether or how you finish your raw edges is totally your call. Everyone who sews has a favorite method. Try different ones to see what suits you best.

HEM OR TURNED EDGE. Useful for straight seam allowances and unfinished outer edges, simply turn under the raw edge once or twice, and stitch.

ZIGZAG STITCH. Using the zigzag stitch, sew every raw edge of each seam with the outside point of the stitch at the edge of the fabric.

PINKING. Pinking is very easy — and it's worth it to invest in some good pinking shears. Just sew a straight line of stitching ½" from the edge. Then use pinking shears to cut off the outer edge.

FRAY PREVENTER. Use this product to seal the cut edges of fabric and prevent it from fraying or unravelling.

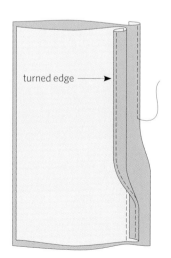

turned edge

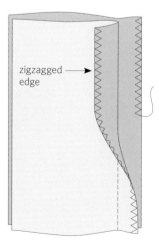

zigzagged edge

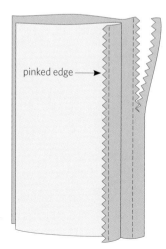

pinked edge

Making a Double-fold Hem

We think of hems as something on the bottom of a skirt or dress, but any raw edge that is not part of a seam, like the edge of a pocket or bag, will need to be hemmed. The best way to do that is with a double-fold hem. Here's how you make one.

1 Press the raw edge ¼" or ½" to the inside.

2 Press under another ½". If you like, put in a few pins to hold the hem in place while you stitch.

3 Stitch as close as you can to the bottom fold, as shown. The bobbin stitches will show on the outside, so choose your thread color accordingly.

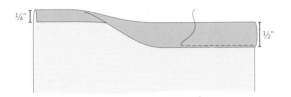

A double-fold hem results in a very clean look with no danger of fraying edges.

Bias Tape Pointers

What is bias tape? Also called *binding*, it's a narrow strip of fabric that has been cut on the bias (at a 45-degree angle to the grain) to give it more stretch. Bias tape not only hides raw edges, it can be a lovely way to add some color and definition to some projects, such as the Simple Slippers on page 74. You can buy it prepackaged at your local fabric shop in a variety of styles (single-fold, double-fold), widths, and colors. You can also make your own.

Attaching Bias Tape

To attach bias tape to a pocket or other raw edge, place the center fold of the bias tape over the top fabric edge and pin it in place. Then edgestitch along the bottom edge of the bias tape. Nothin' to it. Here's a little trick, though: When you look closely at store-bought tape, you'll see that the folded sides are not exactly the same width. This is not a manufacturing error, it's intentional. Put the narrower side on the top of the fabric and the wider side in back. When you stitch along the bottom edge (in front), you will automatically catch the back fold with your stitches. Now isn't that a nifty idea!

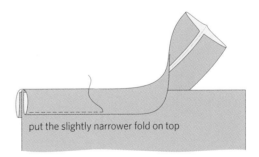

put the slightly narrower fold on top

How to Make Binding or Straps

There isn't much need in this book for making your own bias tape, but you will be making straps from time to time — and both are made the same way. The trick is to figure out how wide to cut the fabric strip, and the rest amounts to folding, pressing, and stitching. Here's what you do:

1 Decide how wide you want the finished strap to be and double that amount; then add enough for folding under the raw edges, usually ½" on each side. (You'll find suggestions in the project instructions.) If making bias tape, decide on the width and multiply by four; the fabric strip will be essentially folded in quarters.

2 For this example, let's say you want to make a 1" strap. Cut a strip of fabric 3" wide x the length you want. True bias strips are cut on the bias to make them flexible; straps don't need to be cut on the bias.

Fold the strip of fabric in half lengthwise, wrong sides together, and press along the fold. Each half will be 1½" wide. Open up the strip, then press under each side ½".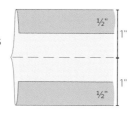

3 Refold the strip with the sides tucked in. If it's binding you're after, you're done. For straps, edgestitch along the length of both sides for greater strength.

Zippers

Projects such as the Box Cushion (see page 105) and the Marshmallow Cushion (see page 117) work best with a zipper for easy insertion and removal of the cushion. Don't worry; putting in a zipper needn't be difficult. One trick is using narrow strips of fusible web to hold the zipper in place (instead of basting) while you stitch. Fusible web is a man-made fiber that will melt when heated. When you place it between two pieces of fabric and press with an iron, the melted web fuses the fabrics together. It comes in many forms, but for zippers you want a roll of ½"-wide tape. Some tapes come with paper on the back and others are just a strip of web. We used the web with paper on the back. Always read the manufacturer's instructions before using, and it's a good idea to test it on a scrap piece of the fabric you're using.

NOTE: *Avoid touching the web directly with the iron, or it will melt onto the iron.*

Here's how to use fusible tape to install a zipper:

1 Select the fabric pieces that will be on either side of the zipper. Lay them facedown on a table, side-by-side. Center the zipper facedown where the fabrics meet, leaving the same amount of fabric above and below the zipper. With chalk or a pencil, mark on the wrong side of the fabric where the zipper pull starts and the zipper ends, then remove the zipper.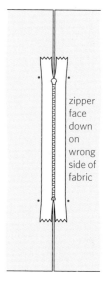

zipper face down on wrong side of fabric

2 Pin the two fabric strips together with right sides facing. Stitch the seam, changing to a basting stitch between the zipper markings and back-stitching on the regular seam above and below the zipper.

3 Press the seam open. With the paper in place and the fusible side facing down, use an iron to apply fusible tape on each seam allowance in the zipper section between the markings. Instead of applying the tape all the way up to the seam, leave a narrow gap where the zipper teeth will go.

4 Peel the paper off the fusible tape and place the zipper facedown on top of it. Fuse the zipper to the seam.

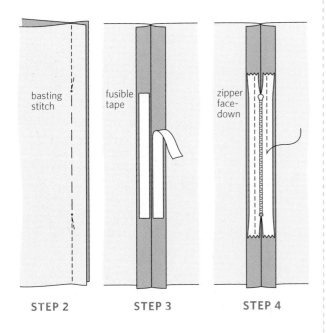

basting stitch

fusible tape

zipper facedown

STEP 2   STEP 3   STEP 4

5 Using a zipper foot, stitch along the sides, top, and bottom of zipper. Flip the fabric over to the right side and use a seam ripper to remove the basting stitches.

Embellishment and Trim

For the most part, I like to keep my home furnishings simple and unfussy, but there are a million ways to add your own personal touch to the projects in this book. Here are a few suggestions for you:

APPLIQUÉ. A cut-out design that is stitched and/or glued onto your project. You can add bits to pillows, place mats, curtains, or whatever you like, for visual impact. The Improv Appliqué Blankie (see page 109), is a good example of how simple shapes can transform a project. You could try appliqué on most of the pillows as well.

BUTTONS. Used primarily for closures, buttons can also be used as decoration.

EMBROIDERY. A design that is hand-sewn or machine-stitched on your project. Some good projects to try this out on might be the Dish Towel (see page 81) or a pocket on the Classic Apron (see page 97).

RIBBON. A colorful strip of ribbon can be used in all kinds of ways: as trim on lamp shades (see Night-Light Lamp Shade Cover on page 115), as a drawstring (see Goodie Bags on page 90), or to hang a project (see Felt Mobile on page 107).

TWILL TAPE. This strip of woven fabric, rather like a heavyweight version of ribbon, can be used for tie closures, straps, or handles. Check out the Mobile Office Tote (see page 135) and the Classic Apron (see page 97). Twill tape is available in different weights, widths, and colors.

PIPING. A tubular band of material, usually wrapped around a cord. Piping can be stitched into seams as an accent trim for upholstery, as on the Bolster Pillows (see page 70). To make your own piping, see Professional Touch on the next page.

PROFESSIONAL TOUCH

Nothing gives a pillow pizzazz like custom-made piping, made from the same fabric as the pillow (or a contrasting color or stripe, if you prefer). All you need is the fabric and some simple cording of a thickness you like.

1 Determine the width of the fabric by multiplying your seam allowance by 2, plus the circumference of your cording.

> TIP: *Wrap the fabric tightly around the cord and measure it.*

2 Cut a strip of fabric this width x the length of the seam where you want piping. For best results, cut along the bias of the fabric, which will give your piping some flexibility for turning corners. If you need a very long strip, you might need to stitch a couple of strips together at the short ends, then press the seams open.

3 Fold the strip in half along its length and tuck the cording into the fold. Use a long stitch length and a zipper foot to stitch very close to the cording, encasing it in the fabric.

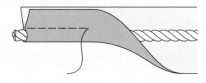

To add piping to the seam of a project, do the following:

1 Pin the piping on the right side of the fabric, with the seam allowance running along the raw edge of the fabric. Clip the piping seam allowance as needed to ease around curves and corners.

2 Machine-baste the piping to the fabric, using a zipper foot and stitching just inside the stitches that hold the piping together.

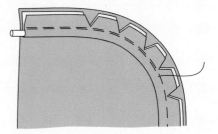

3 Pin the matching fabric, right sides together, on top of basted fabric. Turn the fabrics over and use the basting stitches as a reference for stitching the two fabrics together, stitching slightly to the left of the basting.

Adding buttoned straps to the arms of a loose-fitting slipcover creates a more polished look.

From Drab to Fab

A personal makeover can make you feel like a million bucks.
Something as simple as a new haircut or a new pair of shoes can
make a world of difference. The principle is the same for a home
makeover, whether you're decorating a room from scratch or
replacing just a few elements. Tackle one project at a time and
keep your vision for the whole room in mind as you go along.
A pillow here and a coat of paint there, and you will see and
feel the difference. You may not finish the room overnight, but
you'll use your own personal style and ideas to show off your
personality, taste, and talent.

Entryway

Living Room

Bedroom

39

CHAPTER 4

Inviting Entryway

EVEN IF YOU DON'T HAVE AN ELABORATE FOYER or a lot of extra space when you walk in the door, there are plenty of ways to say "welcome!" Here are three low-sew projects that show what you can do with a bit of inventiveness and a few yards of fabric. Made up in brightly color-coordinated patterns, this covered seat with shelves, catchall tray for keys and accessories, and lightweight floor mat invite residents and visitors alike to pause and catch their breath at the door.

BEFORE

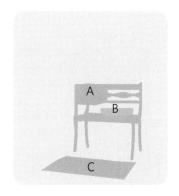

A. *Reupholstered Seat*

B. *Fabric Tray*

C. *Flirty Floor Mat*

Reupholstered Seat

This old "telephone table" was a fun find at an antique shop. It has shelves for phone books, a pad of paper, and a pen for taking messages or doodling. You can paint it, like we did here, or if the piece is in good shape, leave it as is.

Our finished size

15" x 25"

What you'll need

- Chair, bench, or stool with a drop-in seat
- Staple remover, flathead screwdriver, or pliers
- 1½" thick batting or foam
  (see Batting vs. Foam below)
- Electric kitchen knife or serrated knife
  (if using foam)
- 1 yard of cotton batting
- 1 yard of fabric, depending on your seat size
- Spray adhesive (see Safety First! on page 28)
- Staple gun or upholstery tacks

BATTING VS. FOAM

If you're using foam, you only need enough to fit the seat dimensions. Some fabric stores will cut the foam to size for you, so bring your measurements with you when you buy. If you prefer to use batting instead, buy enough to layer it to a depth of 1½", with extra overhang for attaching it to the seat (this can be polyester or whatever is economical). You will need an additional yard of cotton batting for the final layer of padding.

Prepare the bench

1. Unscrew or pop out the seat of your bench or chair. Carefully strip off the fabric by removing the tacks or staples on the underside. If you're short on time or everything is in great shape, you might

just want to cover the entire seat without stripping the old fabric off. When we did this one, there were two layers of fabric underneath: one cloth and one vinyl. Because of the vinyl, we decided to take off both layers.

Measure and cut the materials

2. Cut a piece of thick batting or foam to fit the top of the plywood seat:

   - If you are using batting, cut two or three layers to fit the top exactly and affix them to the seat one layer at a time. Cut the last layer larger, so you can pull the edges around the seat and attach them. If you pull all of the layers over the edges, your cover will be too bulky.

   - If you are using foam, cut it to fit the seat, with an electric kitchen knife or serrated knife.

3. Use the fabric you removed as a template to cut a piece of cotton batting and a piece of the new fabric, adding 2" on all sides.

Cover the seat

4 Spray the plywood seat with adhesive, following manufacturer's directions, and place the thick batting or foam on top of it. Let the adhesive set.

5 Flip the padded seat facedown and center it on the large piece of cotton batting.

- Pull the top edge over to the back of the plywood and staple in place, starting at the center of the side edges and moving out to the corners.

- Do the same on the opposite (bottom) side, again starting at the center and working out to the corners. Be sure to smooth out any wrinkles as you go.

- Trim any excess lumps, especially around the corners, to reduce bulk.

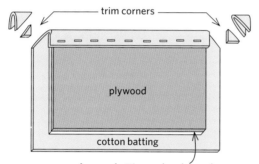

trim corners

plywood

cotton batting

foam or batting under plywood

6 Center the padded seat facedown on the fabric, and attach the fabric in the same way as the batting. Tuck in the corners as you fold them, as if you were wrapping a package, and trim away excess, being careful not to cut too close to the sides.

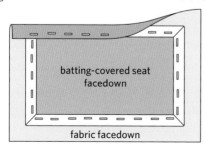

batting-covered seat facedown

fabric facedown

Reassemble the seat

7 Drop the seat back into the frame. Screw it into place, if needed.

Fabric Tray

Creating clear storage is one of the best makeover tricks you'll learn. Baskets and trays can be used for eyeglasses by your bedside, watches and bracelets on your dresser, or remotes in your living room.

Our finished size
Approximately 11" x 16"

What you'll need

- ½ yard of fabric
- ½ yard of double-sided fusible stiff interfacing
- Contrasting thread

TIP

The stiff interfacing can be tough on your needles, so plan to have extras nearby, just in case.

Measure and cut

1 Measure, mark, and cut two 12" x 18" pieces of fabric. Also cut one piece of interfacing the same size.

Fuse the pieces

2 Place the pieces of fabric with wrong sides together and sandwich the interfacing between them. Iron to fuse all three pieces together.

Measure and mark the base

3 Using chalk or a fabric pencil, measure 3¼" from each side and draw a smaller rectangle (approximately 5½" x 11½") inside the main piece. Draw a line from each corner of the outside rectangle to each corresponding corner of the inside rectangle.

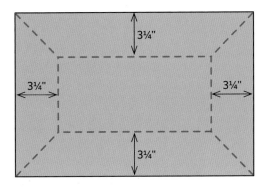

4 Measure and mark a dot 3½" down the diagonal line from each corner. Measure and mark another dot 2" from both sides of each outer corner. Connect the dots as shown.

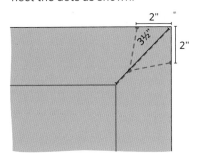

Cut out the corners

5 Cut out the kite-shaped piece you've drawn at each corner.

Stitch the tray

6 Following your markings, zigzag stitch around the inner rectangle to create the base of your tray.

7 Push the corners together and stitch using a tight machine satin stitch.

8 Finish the outer edges of the tray with a tight machine satin stitch.

VARIATION

To make the tray reversible, use two different fabrics: one for the top and one for the bottom. Push the base of the tray in either direction to change the look.

Flirty Floor Mat

This little mat can spruce up your entryway in a snap. Ours is designed to go with the seat and fabric tray, but you could put it in any doorway or room. If you use two prints, it could be reversible, too. We suggest pairing your mat with a nonskid pad. Pretty is nifty, but safe is great!

Our finished size

22" x 32"

What you'll need

♦ ¾ yard of two fabrics, depending on your desired size

TOUGHEN UP!

If you want a mat for your porch or higher-traffic areas, you can add a few coats of polyurethane to the top for a smooth, sweepable surface. (Be sure to test for colorfastness when using polyurethane on fabric.) If you want a more durable mat that's still machine washable, you can also use heavier fabrics like canvas, cotton duck, or denim on both sides.

Measure and cut the fabric

1 To match our size, measure and cut two rectangles from the fabrics:
   - 22" x 32" from the top fabric
   - 25" x 35" from the bottom fabric

   If making your own custom size, cut the top fabric to the desired size and make the bottom fabric 3" larger in both dimensions.

Line up the corners

2 Lay the bottom fabric on a flat surface, wrong side facing up. With wrong sides facing, center the other fabric on top and pin in place. There should be 1½" on all sides of the fabric. Turn under each corner of the bottom fabric and tuck it under the top fabric, so that the folded edge is even with the top corner, as shown.

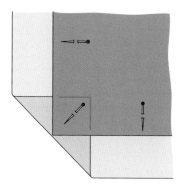

Fold and stitch the edges

3 Fold over and press each edge of the bottom fabric ¾" to meet the edge of the top fabric.

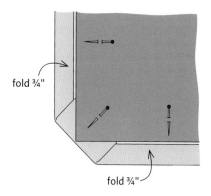

fold ¾"

fold ¾"

4 Fold over and press each edge of the bottom fabric once again, so that the folded fabric neatly encloses each corner. Pin the folded fabric and stitch along the inside folded edge, pivoting at each inside corner. Here's a nice place to use a contrasting color of thread. If you like, add another row of stitching about ¼" inside the first stitching line.

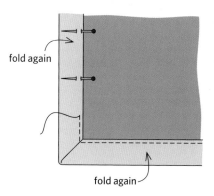

fold again

fold again

BEFORE

CHAPTER 5

La Vida Lively
(Living Room)

THE LIVING ROOM WEARS A LOT OF HATS. It's for relaxing, playing, entertaining, and being entertained. It's full of the comfiest furnishings and the most hi-tech gear in the house. How do we combine those elements, make it look and feel good, and show off our personalities? Start by taking inventory and decide what really needs to go and what can be made over. You'll need to customize the seat covers to fit your own furniture, but the directions here will help give you the confidence and the know-how to make the needed adjustment. And, of course, the look of this room reflects a young, informal aesthetic. Try mixing-and-matching a variety of fabric swatches to find a look that fits your personal aesthetic and the style of your home.

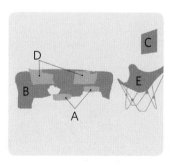

A. *Basket Liner*

B. *Sofa Slipcover*

C. *Stretched Canvas Art*

D. *Envelope Pillows*

E. *Butterfly Chair Cover*

Basket Liner

This is a supereasy project that can add a little zip to a simple basket, whether made of wicker or plastic, even a wooden or metal box or crate. The liners are machine washable, so you can keep 'em fresh. They're so easy to make, you can swap them out whenever you feel like giving a room a little boost.

Our finished size
9" x 5¾" x 3½"

What you'll need
- Basket
- ⅓ yard of fabric, depending on the size of your basket

Measure and cut the fabric

1 For the bottom piece, measure the length and width of the basket bottom, then add 1¼" to each measurement for ease and seam allowance. On the wrong side of the fabric, mark and cut a piece this size (ours was 10¼" x 6").

2 For the sides:
   - Measure around the outside top edge, then add 1¼".
   - Measure from the top lip to the bottom, then add about 3" for the overhang and hem, plus ½" for seam allowance.

Use these dimensions to measure and cut a piece for the sides (ours was 31¾" x 5").

Stitch the liner

3 To make the sides of the liner, stitch a ¼" double-fold hem (see page 34) on one long edge of the side piece, then press. With right sides facing, line up the short raw edges and stitch them together. Press seam open.

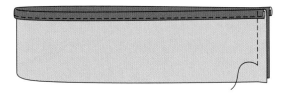

4 Lay the bottom of the liner flat. With right sides facing, line up the side seam in one corner, then pin the strip to the bottom piece. You will need to carefully clip the seam allowance of the strips at the corners so you can pivot and stitch around the corners.

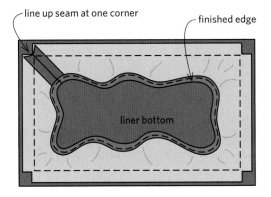

line up seam at one corner

finished edge

liner bottom

Line the basket

5 Insert the liner into the basket and fold the hemmed edge over the top of the basket.

Sofa Slipcover

Since the sofa is the anchor of your living room, it should feel and look terrific. Even the most pitiful sofa can be salvaged with some fabric and creativity. For beginners (and even for some seasoned sewers), the thought of tackling the reupholstery of a sofa is too intimidating. But a casual sofa slipcover like this one is surprisingly forgiving and more flexible than you may think.

What you'll need

- 58/62" upholstery fabric for the slipcover (for yardage estimates, see Winging It below)
- 2 buttons, your choice of size and style
- Upholstery piping (optional), enough for each front arm seam (regular piping is too small)

WINGING IT

Here are some guidelines for fabric shopping. If you're covering a larger-than-average piece, want to cover the cushions separately, or feel like adding a lot of bells and whistles, you'll need more fabric. If your sofa is smaller and your slipcover is simpler, you'll need less. I always lean toward buying more than I need so I can use it for pillows, curtains, or other projects. For large repeat and/or pattern matching, add up to 1 yard for each repeat to ensure proper pattern matching.

SOFA: *15–25 yards*

LOVESEAT: *10–16 yards*

CHAIR: *8–10 yards*

OTTOMAN: *2–5 yards*

What a great way to use your favorite leftover fabric scraps and get organized at the same time!

Measure your sofa

1   Every sofa is different, but most have the same basic structure. The key is to break it down into sections. Measure your sofa using the guidelines provided, then add extra as instructed. When in doubt, measure generously. You'll want to leave plenty of room for tucking and pin-fitting. Believe me, it's easier to trim the fabric if you have too much than it is to recut the whole thing if you don't have enough! (In the instructions below, SA stands for seam allowance.)

- ◆ **A. FRONT** (from back of seat down to the floor) + 9" (5" for tuck, 4" for hem)

- ◆ **B. BACK** (from back of seat up and around to the floor) + 9" (5" for tuck, 4" for hem)

- ◆ **C. BACK WIDTH** (outside width at widest points, excluding arms) + 11" (5" for tuck on each side, 1" for SA)

NOTE: *The width of the back will also serve as the width of the front.*

- ◆ **D. ARMS FRONT WIDTH** (at widest point) + 2" (1" for SA, 1" for ease)

- ◆ **E. ARMS FRONT HEIGHT** + 6" (1" for SA, 1" for ease, and 4" for hem)

- ◆ **F. ARMS SIDE** (from inside deck edge to outside floor) + 9" (5" for tuck, 4" for hem)

- ◆ **G. ARMS SIDE DEPTH** (interior depth) + 4" (1" for SA, 3" for tuck)

- ◆ **H. ARMS BACK WIDTH** + 2" (1" for SA, 1" for ease)

- ◆ **I. ARMS BACK HEIGHT** + 6" (1" for SA, 1" for ease, 4" for hem)

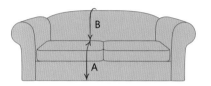

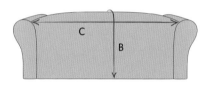

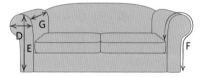

ALTERNATIVES

We chose to cover the entire sofa with the cushions on. If you want to cover the cushions separately, take the cushions off and make the cover to fit without them (in which case you won't need as much fabric for tucking). Then see the instructions for making the Box Cushion on page 105.

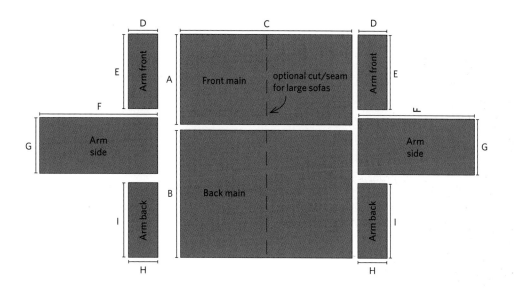

Cut out the pieces

2 Mark the measurements on the wrong side of your
fabric and cut out the pieces. (If you are matching
repeats or using directional fabric, do the marking
on the front side.) Don't worry about any curved
edges yet; those will be addressed later. Cut out
rectangles based on your measurements, as shown
in the cutting diagram. It's a good idea to mark or
label the pieces so you can tell them apart when
you begin stitching them together. The diagram
maps out the basics, but you will need to adapt the
measurements and proportions to fit your sofa.

FOR WIDER SOFAS

**Because our sofa was wider than our 58"-wide fabric,
we made the front and back main panels from two
pieces. To do this, add an inch to the C width for seam
allowance, divide the C width in half, and cut two
pieces for each front and back instead of one.**

3 In addition to the main parts, cut two pieces for
straps across the arms; we cut ours 5" x 15" to
produce two 2"-wide straps.

Stitch the front and back

4 If your front and back main panels require two
pieces, stitch the halves together, right sides facing. Press the seams open.

5 With right sides facing, pin the back and front
panels together along the edges that will form the
back of the seat. If you are using directional fabric,
make sure the pattern is heading in the right direction on both pieces. If your front and back panels
are made from two pieces, match up the center
seams. Stitch and press the seams.

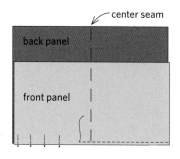

Shape the arms

6 With wrong sides facing out, pin the front arm pieces onto the front arms of the sofa with the extra fabric at the bottom. With a chalk pencil or fabric marker, trace the curve or shape of the arm and trim the fabric as needed, leaving the pieces pinned to the sofa. Only trim the top curve — don't trim to fit the entire arm. Do the same with the arm back pieces. Again, if you are using fabric with a directional repeat or design that needs attention to placement, work from the right side of the fabric.

7 If you want piping, machine-baste it now to the outside raw edges of the arm front pieces on the right side of the fabric. Keep in mind that you don't need piping in the fabric that will be hemmed at the bottom.

8 With wrong sides facing out, place the arm side panels on the sofa. Line up the bottom edges with the front and back arm bottom edges. Start pinning from the floor at one outer front corner; pin up that side and around the curve of the arm to the seat. Repeat on the opposite side of the sofa. Pin the arm side to the arm back in the same way.

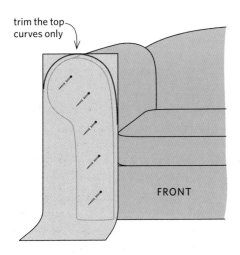

trim the top curves only

FRONT

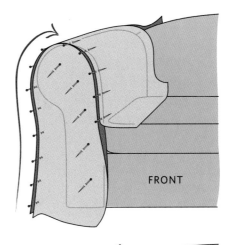

FRONT

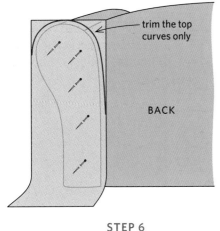

trim the top curves only

BACK

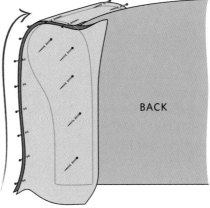

BACK

STEP 6

STEP 8

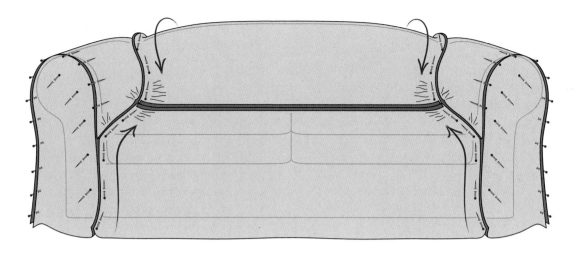

STEPS 9 & 10

Assemble the pieces

9 With wrong side facing up, place the front/back main panel on the sofa, carefully lining up the edges to the seams of the sofa and pushing the extra at the back seam down into the sofa for sitting ease. Begin pinning it to the sides at the bottom front corners; pin up to the back of the seat, pushing what will be the seam down around the cushion for sitting ease, then stop.

10 Pin up the back, starting at the bottom corners and going up and over the top edges. As you pin down to the seat and the seam below it, gather the material in a few folds and pin the seam allowance near the outside edges of the seat to create an easy curve that will fit around the back cushions.

Make the straps

11 Fold one strap piece in half lengthwise. Press, pin, and stitch one short end and the raw long edge. Clip the corners, turn, and press. Repeat with the other strap.

SNIP AND TUCK

You want a fair amount of extra fabric for tucking down behind the sofa cushions and side arms, to prevent tearing the seams when you sit on the sofa. However, if you find that you have more fabric than you need for tucking, now is the time to adjust the fit.

Sit on the sofa to test the amount of sitting ease and then simply move your pins to where you want the seams to be. Once your pins are in place and you are satisfied with the fit, trim the excess fabric, leaving a ½" seam allowance all around.

If you have a lot more than you need, you can trim as needed from the width of the main panel — just be sure to trim evenly from each side so your seam is still in the center of the sofa.

12 Stitch a horizontal buttonhole 1½" from the closed short end of each strap.

Attach the piping and straps

13 On the inner side of each arm, slide the straps between the piping and the front arm panels, lining up the raw edges. Make sure the finished ends are inside and the raw edges are pinned into the seam; otherwise, the strap will go the wrong way when you turn the slipcover.

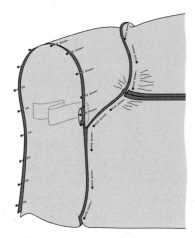

Finish the slipcover

14 Carefully remove the slipcover from the sofa and begin stitching the pieces together, clipping curves as needed and using a zipper foot if you added piping. Follow the same order as when you pinned.

15 Turn the stitched slipcover right side out and put it on the sofa. Tuck fabric in around the seat and back cushions where necessary, then pin the fabric along the bottom edges so the hem will just touch the floor. Remove the slipcover from the sofa, turn wrong side out, and sew the hem. Trim any excess seam allowance, turn right side out, and put the slipcover back on your sofa.

16 One at a time, pull each strap across a front arm and decide how taut you'd like it to be. Mark the button placement on the outer arm side and hand-sew it in place. Ours is loose for a little extra shape, but you can place the button farther out for a tighter fit.

Stretched Canvas Art

You can have all kinds of things printed on to fabric: photos, drawings, illustrations, your own textile designs. Let the fabric tell a story to add some of your own personal flair to the room. For this one, we took a single flower from one of my fabrics (Viona), blew it up, and had it custom printed. We even changed the colors to match the new sofa fabric. Art doesn't have to be expensive, it just needs to be something you like and enjoy. Think out of the box and create your own personal treasures!

Our finished size

20" x 24"

What you'll need

- 1 painter's prestretched canvas
- ¾ yard of fabric (bought, found, or custom printed), or an amount that will fit the canvas plus a few inches
- Several large clips or clamps (optional)
- Staple gun and staples

Stretch the fabric over the canvas

1 Lay your fabric over the stretched canvas, centering the design or motif (or place it where you want, if you prefer not to center it).

2 Flip the canvas over without shifting the placement of the design. You can clip or clamp the fabric in place, if you like, or simply peek under to make sure it hasn't shifted.

Staple into place

3 From the back, fold the top edge of the fabric over the top of the canvas. Use just one or two staples to hold it in place. Move across to the opposite side and pull the fabric taut. Check to make sure the image is where you want it in the front, and again use just a couple of staples. Move to one of the sides and do the same, then do the opposite side last. When the center points are secure, start working your way out to the corners, pulling the fabric taut along the way. Fold the fabric neatly at the corners and staple them last.

THE MORE, THE MERRIER

Another fun way to make stretched fabric art is to group together a bunch of smaller pieces. These can be made in a snap and make quite a statement. It's also a great way to use excess bits of fabric. Embroidery hoops are a quick alternative to stretched canvas. They come in a wide variety of sizes, with wooden and metal finishes that create a framelike effect.

Envelope Pillow

Envelope pillows are great because you can swap them out seasonally or whenever you feel like refreshing the look of a room. Search for a variety of fabrics in varying colors, prints, and textures so you can build a collection of pillows that are fun and comfortable. If your sofa is neutral, you can let the pillows become a focal point and use them to show your sassy side.

Our finished size

16" x 16"

What you'll need

- ◆ ½ yard of fabric, depending on the size of your pillow
- ◆ 1 square pillow form

PILLOW TALK

You can find or make pillows in all shapes and sizes. Mix things up for an eclectic, informal look, or create symmetry with matching pillows at either end if you're going for elegance.

Measure, mark, and cut

1 For the front of the pillow, measure the height and width of your pillow, and add 1" to the measurement. On the wrong side of the fabric, mark and cut one square this size.

2 For the back pieces, you need two rectangles:
- ◆ One side will be the height of the pillow.
- ◆ The other side will be the width of the pillow, plus 3" for overlapping in the center, plus 4" for the hems. Divide that number by two.

Mark and cut out two pieces this size.

Make the back panels

3 On each back piece, make a 1" double-fold hem (see page 34) along one long edge.

Assemble and stitch

4 Assemble the pillow as follows:
- ◆ Lay the front piece on a flat surface, right side facing up.

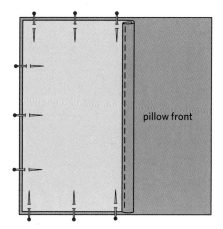

pillow front

- With right sides facing, lay one of the back panels on top, lining up three raw edges, and pin. The hemmed edge should be off center in the middle of the front piece.

- Lay the second back panel on top, lining up raw edges on the opposite side of the front piece. The hemmed edge will overlap the first hemmed edge. Pin the outer edges.

5 Stitch around all outer edges of the pinned pieces. Clip the corners (see page 33).

Insert the pillow form

6 Turn the pillow cover right side out, and use a point turner (see Shortcuts on page 26) to push out all four corners. Insert the pillow form through the opening in the back.

Butterfly Chair Cover

The butterfly chair is a classic. But why be limited to the boring canvas it came with — or the ratty old cover that was on it when you found it at a rummage sale? Use the existing cover as a template and make a brand new seat out of colorful canvas, durable denim, heavy linen, or just about any kind of home décor or upholstery weight fabric. By updating the fabric, the chair now looks like it was made for this living room!

Our finished size

Approximately 38" x 38"

What you'll need

- 1 butterfly chair frame with cover
- 2⅔ yards of fabric for the new cover
- ½ yard of interfacing

GO BOLD!
Use accent pillows to add some punch with complementary or contrasting prints.

Trace and cut the fabric

1 Carefully take apart the old seat cover at the seams. Ours has separate top and bottom pieces (stitched together to form the seat), plus the "pockets" that attach the seat to the chair. If you choose not to take the old seat apart, and are using the stitched pieces as templates, remember to add a ½" seam allowance as needed.

2 Lay the pieces on the wrong side of the new fabric and cut out the following. If your chair is made differently, follow your own template pieces. Our

chair is made with two layers of fabric (two sets of upper and lower pieces) sewn together and turned right side out.

- ◆ 2 upper pieces
- ◆ 2 lower pieces
- ◆ 4 inner pockets, plus 4 pieces of interfacing (the straight edge of our inner pockets are a couple of inches shorter than the outer pockets and added for strength)
- ◆ 4 outer pockets, plus 4 pieces of interfacing

Make and attach the pockets

3 Fuse the interfacing to the wrong sides of the pocket pieces with a hot iron. Make a ¼" double-fold hem along the straight edges of the outer pockets. The inner pockets won't show, so no hem is necessary.

4 With both wrong sides facing up, baste the outer pockets on top of the inner pockets with a ¼" seam allowance. If your chair doesn't have inner pockets, skip this step.

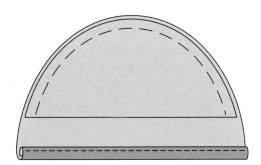

5 Select one upper piece and one lower piece to be the back of the chair. Lay them out flat, and with both right sides facing up, pin the double pockets to each of the corner curves. Stitch in place with a ½" seam allowance.

Stitch the pieces together

6 Starting with the back pieces with pockets, pin the upper and lower pieces right sides together and stitch along the inner curve. Press the seam open; clip a little bit if needed to get it to lie flat.

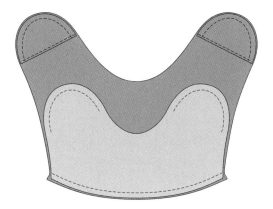

7 To reinforce the seam, cut a strip of interfacing the length of the seam and a bit wider than the pressed seam allowance. Fuse it to the wrong side of the pressed seam.

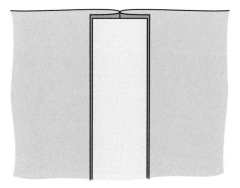

8 Turn over the stitched pieces to the right side and topstitch ¼" on both sides of the seam.

9 Repeat steps 6 through 8 with the remaining upper and lower pieces; this will be the front side of the chair.

10 With right sides together, stitch the back and front panels together, leaving an 8" opening along one side. Turn right side out and press, tucking in the seams along the opening. Edgestitch about ⅛" from the outside edge all the way around, stitching the opening closed in the process.

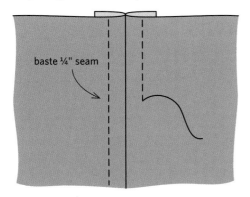

baste ¼" seam

11 Slip the new cover into place and take a seat. You've earned a break!

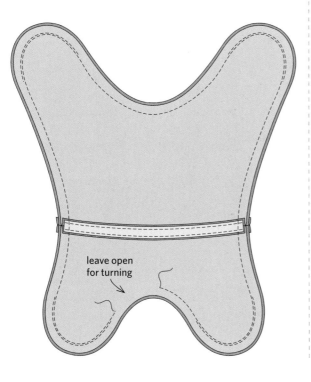

leave open for turning

RE-COVER IT!

Replacing a cover on a butterfly chair, folding organizer (shown above), or anything with fabric cover is easy. Just remove the existing cover and use it as a template for cutting out a new one.

BEFORE

CHAPTER 6

Sweet Dreams Bedroom

FOR THIS MAKEOVER, we wanted the bedroom to feel peaceful and relaxing. But if you want to paint the ceiling purple or hang beaded lights around the bed, I say go for it! Just remember, no matter how much fun you like to have in your room during the day, you will eventually have to sleep in it, so be careful when using stimulating colors and textures. Window treatments present a great opportunity to use the features of fabric to their utmost, depending on the effect you want to achieve. A heavier fabric in a darker color or dramatic print will make a stronger statement, and offer more privacy and light blocking, while a lighter or sheer fabric in softer colors or prints (such as the linen used here) will have a more mellow, soothing effect.

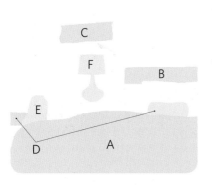

A.   *Dreamy Duvet Cover*

B.   *Upholstered Headboard*

C.   *Roman Shade*

D.   *Bolster Pillows*

E.   *Japanese Yukata Robe and Simple Slippers*

F.   *Fabric-Covered Lamp Shade (see box on page 75)*

Dreamy Duvet Cover

Transform your bed into a fluffy, soft cloud of comfort by topping it with a glorious duvet. We used a flat king sheet and three wide strips of a fabric we loved, but you can select several fabrics instead of one and piece them together, if you prefer. Just remember to cut your strips wide enough for a seam allowance on each side, to keep the top panel the right size.

What you'll need

- 1 flat sheet close to the size of your duvet cover
- 44/45"-wide fabric(s) of choice (see Fabrics and Sizes below)
- Seven ½" buttons (you might use fewer buttons, depending on the size of your duvet)
- Four 14" strips of twill tape (optional)

FABRICS AND SIZES

Below are some guidelines for common duvet cover sizes (the first number is the width), and the total amount of fabric you'll need for each size. The fabric is sewn in three strips, running across the width of the duvet; if you want to use different fabrics for each strip, use the width of the duvet to calculate the yardage for each strip. However, duvet and sheet dimensions vary, depending on the manufacturer, so check for size before you buy the sheet or the fabric. The sheet should be larger than the duvet cover on all sides by at least a couple of inches; see the instructions for when and how to cut the sheet to size.

TWIN SIZE (68" x 88") = 5⅞ yards of fabric

DOUBLE/FULL SIZE (78" x 90") = 6⅝ yards of fabric

QUEEN SIZE (88" x 90") = 7½ yards of fabric

KING SIZE (106" x 92") = 9 yards of fabric

Measure and cut

1 Cut three lengths of 44/45" fabric to match the width of your duvet cover plus 1" for seam allowances and 1" for ease.

WHY ADD EASE?

Since a duvet isn't completely flat, a little extra is added to the measurements to allow for the depth of the duvet. This is so the duvet won't bunch up at the sides inside the cover.

2 To determine the width of each strip of fabric, divide the length of the duvet cover by three, then:

- To two of the strips, add 1" for seam allowance and 1" for ease.
- To the third strip add 1" for seam allowance, 1" for ease, and 2" for the hemmed opening. This strip will be at the bottom of the duvet cover.

Cut each of the three fabric strips to the correct width. Put a safety pin on the bottom edge of the wider/bottom fabric strip to keep track of where the hem will go.

Stitch the duvet cover top

3 With right sides facing, pin the two same-size fabric strips together along one long raw edge, then stitch. In the same way, pin and stitch the bottom fabric to the other strips along one long edge.

FABRIC TIP

When pinning and stitching the pieces together, be sure to pay attention to the direction of the print, so all three pieces have the pattern going in the same direction.

4 Press the two seam allowances toward the bottom of the cover. Edgestitch the seam allowances in place.

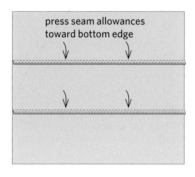

press seam allowances toward bottom edge

Make the buttonholes

5 Lay the stitched fabrics on top of the sheet, lining up the wider hemmed edge of the sheet with the bottom of the wider fabric strip. Without cutting the wide-hemmed edge, trim the sheet to the same size as the stitched fabrics. Set the stitched top aside.

6 Mark the placement of vertical buttonholes along the hemmed edge of the sheet. Measure about 15" from each side and make a mark. (You will be stitching from these points in step 11.) Evenly distribute the buttonholes between these two measurements, about ½" from the finished edge. It helps to place the center button first, halfway between the 15" marks. Stitch the buttonholes and clip them open.

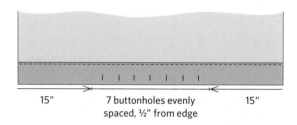

15"   7 buttonholes evenly   15"
spaced, ½" from edge

SNUG BUTTONHOLES

The buttonholes should be slightly shorter than the circumference of your buttons to ensure a tight fit.

7 Press under the hemmed edge 2" to hide the buttonholes. Machine-baste or hand-sew a vertical row of stitches ¼" from each side edge to hold the fold in place. Don't worry about seeing the stitches; they'll be hidden by the seam allowance later. Set the sheet aside.

Attach the buttons

8 On the stitched fabric panels, make a 1" double-fold hem (see page 34) on the bottom edge (where you placed the safety pin). The stitched fabric piece should now be the same size as the sheet.

9 With right sides together, lay the sheet on the stitched fabrics, lining up the hemmed edges. To determine where the buttons will go, push a straight pin through the center of each buttonhole through all layers to the wrong side of the fabric.

Mark this point with a fabric marker. Hand-sew the buttons in place on the wrong side of the fabric. (Buttonholes and buttons will both be on the inside of the duvet cover.)

Stitch the sides

10 With right sides together, line up the hemmed edges and pin the sheet and the stitched fabrics together along the sides and one end. If your duvet has loops at the corners, you can add twill tape to the corners of the duvet cover, to tie the corners and keep the duvet from sliding inside the cover. Simply fold the twill tape strips in half and pin the folded edge in the corners as shown.

11 On the hemmed edges, pin from the 15" marks to the corners on both sides. Starting at one of the 15" marks, backstitch and then edgestitch to the nearest corner, as close as possible to the hemmed edges. Pivot at that corner and stitch a ½" seam all the way down the side, around the end, and down the side to the opposite hemmed edge. Pivot at the last corner and edgestitch 15", then backstitch. Trim all corners, turn right side out, and press.

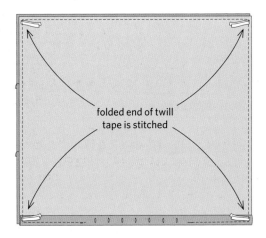

folded end of twill tape is stitched

12 Insert the duvet, pushing into all four corners (and tying the twill tape in the loops, if you have them). Button the opening closed.

Upholstered Headboard

A great way to add comfort and style to your bedroom is with a custom, no-sew headboard. Whether you like to sit up and read, or cozy up to watch a movie, a comfy headboard will make your evenings more relaxing. You can even use an upholstered headboard with a frame or dress up a mattress and box spring right on the floor. Either way, the look is tailored and finished. You can get creative and add tufts or buttons or other embellishments — or you can keep it simple. It's entirely up to you.

Our finished size
72" x 24" x 3½" deep

What you'll need
- ½"-thick plywood (see Hardware Particulars on next page)
- 1x4s (see step 2 for length)
- 2"-thick foam, enough to cover the headboard
- Electric kitchen knife or serrated knife
- 2¼ yards of fabric, depending on headboard size
- 2¼ yards of poly batting
- 2¼ yards of cotton batting
- Staple gun and ⅜" staples
- Spray adhesive (see Safety First! on page 28)
- Drill and drill bits
- Eight 1½" wood screws

With bed frame
- 4 bolts and nuts to fit the holes in the bed frame
- Adjustable wrench

Without bed frame
- Stud finder (if attaching headboard to the wall)
- Level (optional)
- Six 2½" wood screws
- Eight 1½" wood screws
- Phillips head drill bit for screws

Measure and cut the pieces

1   To determine the finished size of your headboard:

  ◆ Measure the width of your bed frame (or your mattress, if you don't use a frame).

  ◆ Measure from the top of your mattress to the height you want the headboard to be. A good gauge is to measure at least 8" higher than your pillows would be if you were sitting up in bed.

  Mark these dimensions onto your plywood and cut it to size. Set aside.

2   To determine the length of the 1×4s:

  ◆ Measure from the floor to the top of the mattress.

  ◆ Measure the height of the headboard and subtract 7".

  Add these two measurements together and cut two pieces this length, then set aside.

3   Measure, mark, and cut the foam to the exact same size as your headboard, using an electric or serrated knife. (Or ask your local supplier to cut it to size for you.)

Plywood is sold in large sheets, typically 4' x 8'. You can buy a sheet and cut it out yourself with a jigsaw or you can have the lumberyard or home improvement store cut it for you (recommended). Ours is 2' x 6' and we cut it ourselves.

4   You want to cut enough fabric and batting to wrap about 4" around to the back on all sides, so add 8" to both measurements in step 1. (Part of that 4" is to allow for the thickness of the foam and batting.) Mark these dimensions on the wrong side of the fabric and cut out the piece.

5   Cut both battings 1½" smaller than the fabric.

Cover the headboard

6   In a well-ventilated area, use spray adhesive to attach the foam to the front of the headboard. Allow it to dry.

7   Lay the poly batting out flat and center the headboard on top, foam side facing down. Fold the edges of the batting around to the back of the headboard and staple in place. Start at the center of the top edge and work to the corners, then do the opposite side, smoothing the batting out as you go. Do the sides last; trim away extra bulk at the corners. Attach the cotton batting in the same way.

8   Attach the fabric in the same way as the battings, pulling the edges to the back of the plywood, folding them under ½", and stapling in place. Start at the top edge, then do the opposite side, pulling the fabric taut as you go and checking to see that any designs are straight and the fabric is pulled evenly to the back. Do the sides last, neatly tucking and folding the corners.

Attach the legs (with a bed frame)

9　Hold the legs, one at a time, up to the preexisting holes or slots in the bed frame and mark where you need to drill holes in the legs. Remove the legs and drill holes (to match the size of the bolts) for attaching the legs to the bed frame. Also drill two sets of screw holes in both legs:

- ◆ 2" from the top and 2" apart
- ◆ 2" from the bottom of the headboard and 2" apart

The double placement of screws ensures that the wood won't warp or curl over time.

NOTE: *Get a friend to help you with the next step.*

10　Attach the legs to the bed frame, using nuts and bolts. Use a wrench to tighten the bolts. Have your friend hold the headboard in place while you attach it to the legs using 1½" screws.

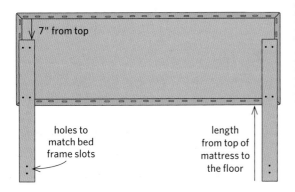

7" from top

holes to match bed frame slots

length from top of mattress to the floor

Attach the legs (without a bed frame)

9　If you don't have a bed frame, you will need to attach the headboard directly to the wall. First you need to locate studs in the wall:

- ◆ Place the headboard, wrong side facing out, at the head of the bed. Use a stud finder to locate the studs in the wall. Use a pencil to mark the center of two different studs.
- ◆ Lay the 1x4s on the headboard, centering them on your markings. Trace along the sides of both to mark their placement. Depending on the location of the studs, your legs might not be evenly spaced on the headboard. That's okay. What's important is that the legs are securely attached to the studs in the wall.

10　Move the headboard to a flat, level surface (the floor is fine) and place it wrong side up. Following your markings, position the 1x4s into place, 7" from the top edge of the headboard. Mark the following spots on the 1x4s for pilot holes:

- ◆ 2 holes: 2" from the top and 2" apart
- ◆ 2 holes: 2" from the bottom of the headboard and 2" apart
- ◆ 1 hole 2" up from the bottom edge of the 1x4s
- ◆ 1 hole 2" down from the bottom edge of the headboard
- ◆ 1 hole in the center of those two (optional, for extra security)

11　Using a Phillips head drill bit and 1½" wood screws, attach both 1x4s to the headboard.

12　Move the bed out of the way and ask a friend to hold the headboard in place, making sure the legs are centered on the studs. Place a level along the top edge of the headboard to make sure it is straight. Secure the legs to the wall with 2½" wood screws. Slide the bed back into place against the headboard.

Roman Shade

This unlined Roman shade is relaxed and informal. Depending on what kind of fabrics you choose, you can keep it casual or make it more tailored and crisp. Roman shades look pretty tricky and can send even the boldest sewer running for the hills. But the truth is: They're not that hard. Just lay out your materials and fabric, then slowly go through the steps. You'll be amazed at how easy it is, once you get started!

Our finished size

30" x 51" when fully opened

What you'll need

- Fabric, enough for the shade and to cover the mounting board (see steps 1 and 2)
- Wood board for mounting the shade
- Staple gun and staples
- ½"-wide Velcro as long as width of shade
- Plastic cord lock pulley (also called Roman shade pulley)
- 3 screw eyes
- Four ⅜"-wide flat dowels or battens
- 8 plastic rings or clips, ½" or ⅝"
- Cord to fit the cord pulley, (⅜" to ¼", the length of the shade x 4 (about 8 yards)
- 3 Phillips head wood screws at least 2" long and drill bit to match

---

WHAT IS A MOUNTING BOARD?

A mounting board is simply the strip of wood that provides the support for the top of the shade. It doesn't have to be a specific thickness, but it needs to be strong enough to hold the weight of the curtain. Ours was ½" x ¾".

Measure and cut the fabric

1   For the shade fabric dimensions, measure the inside width and length of the window frame and do the following:

- add 4" to the inside width of the window frame (for hems)
- add 7" to the length from the top to the sill (for dowel channels and hems)

Mark a rectangle this size on the wrong side of the fabric, and cut it out. Set it aside.

2   For the mounting board length, subtract ½" from the inside width of the window frame. This is so the mounting board will easily fit inside the frame after being wrapped in fabric. Cut the board to this length. Cut a piece of fabric that is 3" longer than the board and wide enough to wrap the board on all sides in fabric.

Prepare the mounting board

3 Lay the long strip of fabric wrong side up and center the board on top, with the wider side of the board facing the fabric. Pull the top edge of fabric down over the board, staple it in place, then pull the bottom edge of fabric up over the board and staple in place. Wrap the short ends over the side edges and staple in place.

4 Attach the hook side of Velcro to the front of the mounting board (opposite the stapled side) with your staple gun.

5 On the bottom side of the board, measure and attach the following, as shown:

- The left side of the cord lock pulley should be about ½" from the left edge.
- Position the first screw eye about 4" from the edge of the pulley, with a second screw eye 6½" from the end near the pulley.
- Place the third screw eye 6½" from the other end of the batten.

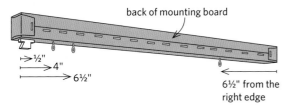

back of mounting board

½"
4"
6½"

6½" from the right edge

Stitch the shade

6 With the wrong side facing up, press under a 1" double-fold hem (see page 34) on both sides of the shade. Stitch.

7 Press under a ½" double-fold hem on the top edge and stitch. Pin a strip of loop Velcro (to match the hook strip on the mounting board) along the top edge of the shade. Stitch in place.

8 For the bottom channel, press under a ¾" double-fold hem on the bottom edge, and stitch, back-stitching at the ends.

RIGHTIE, LEFTIE

We designed our pulleys so the shade pull will be on the right side of the finished shade (remember, the diagram is from the back of the shade). If you want the shade pull on the left of the finished shade, reverse the instructions.

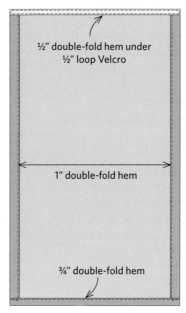

½" double-fold hem under ½" loop Velcro

1" double-fold hem

¾" double-fold hem

STITCHING THE SHADE

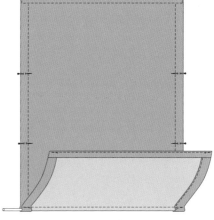

MAKING DOWEL CHANNELS

Make the dowel channels

9   With the right side facing up, use tailor's chalk to mark the shade into four equal sections, horizontally, starting below the hem on the top edge. Use pins to mark location of the dowel channels on each side.

NOTE: *This shade has four folds, but you may want more or fewer folds, depending on your window height.*

10   Starting at the bottom, fold up the fabric at the first set of pins and press. Mark a line ¾" above the pressed fold. Stitch along that line to form a channel for the first dowel. Repeat for the other two dowel channels. Insert dowels into all four channels.

Add the cords

11   Attach the shade to the front of the batten by pressing the two Velcro strips together. Attach two columns of plastic clips or rings to the back of each dowel channel, directly beneath the second and third screw eyes. Measure to make sure they form straight lines. If you are using clips, they'll slide right on to the dowel. If you are using rings, you'll need to hand-sew them in place.

12   Cut two lengths of cord that are three times the length of the window, then do the following:

   ◆ Starting at the side without the cord lock pulley, insert a length of cord into the lowest plastic clip or ring and double-knot the end. Thread the cord up through the clips or rings all the way to the screw eye at the top of that column. Continue threading the cord through the next two screw eyes and into the cord lock pulley.

ANOTHER WAY TO SECURE THE CORDS

Instead of a cord lock pulley you can simply thread the cords up the clips or rings, then through the screw eyes, as described. After the third screw eye, attach the cord pulls and knot the cord ends. You will need to attach a metal or plastic cleat to the window frame for wrapping the cord at desired height.

   ◆ Insert the other length of cord through the other bottom clip or ring and double-knot the end. Thread it up through the clips or rings and through the screw eye at the top of that column, then through the last screw eye and into the cord lock pulley.

Both cords will now be threaded through the cord lock pulley, ready to be pulled together to raise and lower the shade. Add the cord pulls and knot the ends of your cord.

Install the shade

13   Pull apart the Velcro strips to separate the shade from the mounting board. Center the mounting board on the top window frame, with the Velcro side facing you. Drill three holes (in a size to match the wood screws) at even distances across the board through the window frames and into the wood above inside the wall. Using wood screws, attach board to window frame with Velcro side out. Then finger-press top of shade to Velcro on mounting board and adjust cords so shade is at desired height.

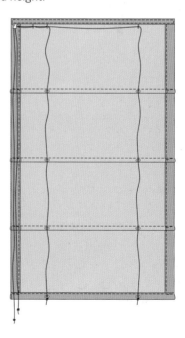

Bolster Pillows

Because we wanted to keep our room serene, these bolster pillows are very simple — no zippers, piping, or other trim — but you can certainly dress 'em up if you like.

Our finished size

6" diameter x 14" long

What you'll need

- 1¼ yard of fabric for 2 bolsters, depending on your bolster size
- 2 bolster pillow forms (see Project Notes at right)

Measure the form

1 Measure across the circular end (the diameter) and add 1" for seam allowance. For the body of the bolster, measure the length, then measure around the cylinder (circumference). Add 1" to each measurement.

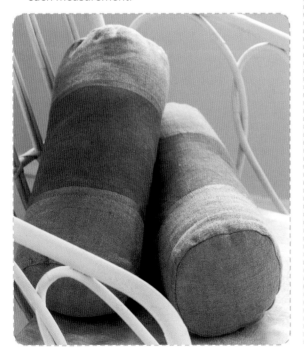

PROJECT NOTES

We used a poly-filled form for these bolsters because we like that the inserts can be manipulated into place even if the cover isn't perfect. If you are using a poly-filled form, it's a good idea to measure the circumference closer to the ends than the middle. The filling can pouf and shift, making it hard to get an accurate measurement in the middle.

Measure and cut the fabric

2 On the wrong side of the fabric, measure and mark two circles for the ends of each bolster (ours is 7"). Use a compass or trace a small plate, if you can find one the right size. Cut out the pieces.

3 Measure and mark a rectangle (length x circumference) for each bolster (ours is 15" x 20"). Cut out the pieces.

Stitch the bolsters

4 If you want piping, refer to box at right. Otherwise, staystitch ½" from the edge around each fabric circle and cut notches 1" apart around the edges. Be careful not to cut beyond stitching. Do the same on the long edges of the rectangles (these long edges will be stitched around the circle).

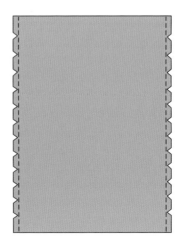

5 With right sides facing, fold each rectangle in half with the notched edges at the ends. Pin and then stitch, leaving an 8" opening with backstitching on both sides.

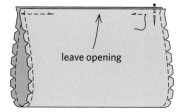

leave opening

6 Before pinning the ends of the cylinders to the circles, you might want to mark points to line up. For instance, fold each circle in half and mark the edges on the fold points. Fold in the opposite direction and mark those fold points. You'll then have marks, as on a clock face, at 12, 3, 6, and 9 o'clock. Do the same with the circular ends of each cylinder.

7 With right sides facing and wrong sides out, pin one of the cylinders to a circle, lining up the marks. Stitch right over the staystitching. Repeat with the remaining cylinder and circles.

Insert the form

8 Turn the cylinders right side out and insert the bolster form through the opening. Hand-sew the opening closed.

NICE PIPES!

If you'd like to add piping around the ends, go for it. You can make your own (see page 37) or you can buy pre-made piping. Machine-baste the piping to the circles on the seamline with the raw edges toward the seam allowance of the circle, using a zipper foot. Then also use a zipper foot to stitch the cylinder to the circles.

Japanese Yukata Robe

Nothing says "luxury" like a fresh, comfy robe. A traditional Japanese yukata is made from lightweight cotton, but ours is made from a repurposed tablecloth! See what you have in your linen closet before rushing out to order fancy, new material. Not a pack rat? Try a local flea market or tag sale to look for suitable and surprising materials to work with. You don't need a fussy pattern to make it, either. Just map it out and jump right in.

Finished size

Can be customized

What you'll need

- One 60" x 104" tablecloth (see Fabric Notes below)
- 1 yard of complementary fabric for the sash

FABRIC NOTES

Depending on your height and the length of your arms, the tablecloth size we recommend may or may not be sufficient. To make sure you have enough fabric, have a friend help you measure in two directions:

- Stretch your arms out horizontally and measure from wrist to wrist. If you want sleeves that will go down to your wrists, the fabric needs to be at least this wide, plus enough for ease and sleeve hems.
- Measure from the top of one shoulder down to the floor, and multiply by two. The fabric needs to be at least this long, plus enough for hems.

If you need or want to buy fabric instead, 3 yards of 54" might do it, if the width of the fabric is enough for your desired sleeve length. A backup plan, if you have long arms, would be to baste two 44" fabrics together along the selvage and map out the robe with a seam down the center back.

Measure and mark the fabric

1 Measure from shoulder to shoulder across your back, and add 8" to 10".

2 Lay the tablecloth/fabric on a flat surface with the right side facing up, then fold it in half crosswise with right sides facing. On the fold and the bottom edge, find and mark the vertical centerline. Mark the shoulder width along the top folded edge of the fabric, with an equal amount on both sides of the centerline.

3 Make another set of marks 10" directly below each shoulder point.

   ◆ If making Western sleeves, draw a line from these points straight out to the sides.

   ◆ If making traditional sleeves, mark another set of points 8" to 10" directly below these points and draw the sleeves as shown.

4 To mark the sides of the robe, draw lines from the shoulder points to the bottom edges.

folded edge   shoulder width + 8" to 10"

10"

8"–10"

Western-style sleeves

traditional sleeves

Cut out and stitch the sides

5 Starting at the bottom edge, cut along your lines through both layers up to the 10" mark. Then start at the side edges and cut in to the lower marks you made for whichever sleeve style you've chosen.

6 Pin the sides and sleeves right sides together and stitch. For traditional sleeves, start at the bottom edge, stitch up to the higher mark, turn a tight corner, and stitch down to the lower mark. Pivot at the lower corner and stitch across to the side edge. Clip the seam allowance on curved edges and corners (see page 33).

Cut out the neckline

7 Create the neckline by marking 4" on both sides of the centerline at the top folded edge. Make a mark on the centerline 2¼" down from the top, and another 3" down from the top. Connect the center neckline marks to the 4" marks as shown to make two semicircles. The higher one will be the back neckline and the lower one will be the front neckline.

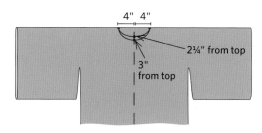

8   Cut out the shorter semicircle through both layers of fabric, then cut out the lower semicircle on the front layer only.

Stitch the front and neckline

9   Starting at the bottom front edge, cut up along the centerline. Pin and stitch a ¼" double-fold hem (see page 34), starting at the bottom edge and going up both side edges, stopping at the neckline. Then make a ¼" double-fold hem around the neckline. Go slowly and use as many pins as you need.

10 To make the V neckline, make a mark about 14" down from the front neckline on the wrong side. Fold over about 3" of the curved neckline on a diagonal to that mark, as shown. Press and stitch along the edge, leaving the inverted collar loose.

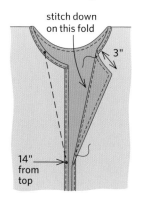

11 If you used a finished tablecloth, you may already have hemmed edges at the sleeves and bottom of the robe. If not, trim and hem the edges as needed to obtain the desired length. Turn the robe right side out and press.

Make the sash

12 To figure out how long your sash needs to be, find a long piece of cording or string. Starting in front, wrap it around your waist to the back, bring both ends back to the front, and tie as you would tie the sash. Measure how much cording you need to do this and add 4" for seam allowances.

13 Since the sash is very long, you'll need to cut it in sections, and it's best to make a template for the pieces. Measure once around your waist and do the following:

◆ The center piece should be 6" x more than half of your waist measurement. This is personal preference, based on how far around your sides you want the widest part of the sash to go. Draw a rectangle to these measurements, then measure 1¼" from the top on both sides. Sketch a curved line from the side marks up along the top edge to the mark. Hint: Fold the paper in half and cut the top curve once, so it will match on both sides. Cut two pieces from fabric.

◆ For the length of the sash ends, subtract the width of the center piece you just made from the cord length and divide by two. Measure out a piece this long that is 5¾" wide on one end and 2½" wide on the other. Cut four pieces from fabric.

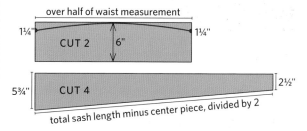

14 With right sides facing, stitch two end pieces to the sides of one center piece. Press seams open. Do the same with the remaining center piece and ends. Pin these two pieces right sides together and stitch on all sides, leaving a 5" opening for turning. Clip the corners and trim the seam allowances, then turn the sash right side out. Tuck the seam allowances into the opening and press. Stitch ¼" from the edge on all sides, closing the opening in the process.

Simple Slippers

Lay out a pair of handmade slippers to welcome you when you get up in the morning. You can match the slippers to the décor of the room, like we did, or to your favorite PJs, or just choose a fabric that's soft and cozy. Think of these slippers as a home improvement for your feet!

Our finished size

10½" long

What you'll need

- ¼ yard of fabric for the foot beds
- ¼ yard of fabric for the uppers
- ¼ yard of toweling, other plush fabric, or batting
- 2½ yards
- Coordinating bias tape, approximately 1¼ yard per slipper

A WELCOMING TOUCH

Don't underestimate the power of comfy slippers. Keep a basket by your front door and guests will instantly feel at home. This project calls for tracing your own foot, but if you are expecting guests with feet of different shapes and sizes, take tracings from a few friends.

Make the templates

1   On a piece of paper, trace around one foot. Smooth out the shape to make it more of an oval than a contoured foot. Draw another shape ½" wider than the first one on all sides (for wiggle room). This template is for the foot bed.

2   For the upper shape, measure and mark the following points around your foot bed template and connect the dots to create a long bell shape:

- 1 point at the top, ½" away from the top of the template
- 2 points, one on either side of the template as shown, 2" from the bottom edge
- 2 points 1½" from both side edges, about midway between top and bottom
- 1 point 6" from the top

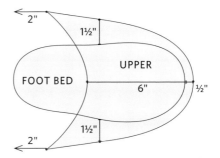

3   Make copies of your drawings and cut out one foot bed template and one upper template.

Cut the fabric

4   Using the foot bed template, cut the following (for two slippers):

- 2 pieces from fabric
- 2 pieces from the padding fabric
- 2 pieces of nonskid fabric for the soles

5 Using the uppers template, cut out 2 pieces, making them ¼" larger than the template to allow for seam allowance.

Assemble the foot beds

6 Layer the pieces for both slippers on a flat surface, as follows:

- ◆ first is the nonskid fabric, right side facing down
- ◆ next is the padding fabric
- ◆ last is the slipper fabric, right side facing up

7 With a ruler and fabric pen or chalk, draw diagonal lines 1" apart across the top fabric. Trace lines on the other top fabric in the opposite direction. Stitch along the lines through all three foot bed pieces. Trim any loose threads and the edges, if they aren't lined up neatly. Set aside.

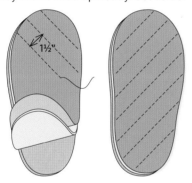

Attach the uppers

8 Before attaching the uppers, finish each lower raw edge with bias tape (see page 34). Trim the ends to line up with the side edges.

9 Position each upper panel on top of a foot bed. Pin in place around the raw edges and baste together.

10 Pin bias tape around the entire edge of each slipper, folding under the ends. Stitch in place.

NOTE: *For stronger slippers, or simply for looks, you might want to add a second row of stitching all around the slippers.*

INSTANT GRATIFICATION

Want to light up a room fast? You can easily transform a space with a quickie lamp shade cover. It takes no sewing and very little time. Just trace, cut, and glue! To make one for your bedroom, just follow instructions for the Night-Light Lamp Shade Cover on page 115. Feel free to embellish the ends with ribbon, fringe, buttons, cording, or whatever turns you on.

Dressing the Table to Fit the Occasion

Whether you are enjoying the morning paper and a café au lait, hosting a cocktail party, or entertaining a crowd for a sit-down dinner, you can find plenty of ways to dress up your table to make it warm and inviting. Here are three ways to make over a room — without changing anything more than what's on the table. Simply swapping out napkins can change the whole tone of the meal and a tablecloth can make over an entire room. Consider the occasion, the space, and your needs, then whip up something to make your events memorable.

A Swell Affair

Party On

Tea for Two

CHAPTER 7

Tea for Two

START OFF YOUR DAY OR WEEKEND by setting a happy scene at the table. Mix-and-match place settings are such an easy and fun way to enjoy your favorite fabrics on a daily basis and only require the simplest of sewing skills. Here's a place where you can be bold in combining patterns that you might not put together in a garment or window treatment. But they look great sitting next to each other as napkin and place mat. The addition of a few handmade amenities can turn an ordinary morning ritual into special, quality time with a doting partner or dear friend. Tea and crumpets or bagels and cream cheese — you choose the menu and you design the ambiance!

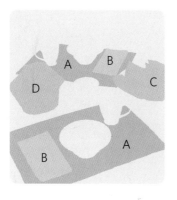

A. *Reversible Place Mats*

B. *Unlined Napkins*

C. *Dish Towel*

D. *Tea Cozy*

Reversible Place Mats

A simple continental breakfast can feel positively posh when you set your plate atop a handsome place mat. Making them reversible allows for quickie makeovers whenever the mood strikes you. If you like a unified look, use the same fabric to stitch up the napkins in the next project, too. We matched them up, but you don't need to follow suit. For an eclectic look, use a variety of fabrics.

Our finished size

14½" x 20½"

What you'll need

- ½ yard each of two fabrics, per place mat
- ½ yard of fusible interfacing, per place mat

Measure and cut

1 On the wrong side of each fabric, measure and mark a 15½" x 21½" rectangle. Cut one piece of interfacing the same size.

Fuse the interfacing

2 Fuse the interfacing to the wrong side of the fabric piece, following manufacturer's directions.

Stitch the place mats

3 Pin the two fabric pieces with right sides together and the interfaced side faceup. Stitch around the raw edges, leaving a 6" opening on one long side.

4 Clip the corners (see page 32) and turn the fabrics right side out. Push out the corners with a point turner, and tuck the seam allowance neatly into the opening. Press.

5 Edgestitch about ⅜" from the outer edge all the way around, stitching the opening closed in the process.

Unlined Napkins

I absolutely love cloth napkins on a table. They make even the simplest meal feel festive and worth savoring. And napkins are just as satisfying to make as they are to use. They take very little time and make such a difference on the table. We made ours to match the reversible place mats, so we can flip the mats and mix up the napkins, yet still have a coordinated look.

Our finished size

19" square

What you'll need

◆ 1¼ yard of fabric will make 4 napkins

Measure and cut the fabric

1   On the wrong side of the fabric, measure and mark four 20" squares.

2   Use a rotary cutter and mat, or a yardstick and scissors, to cut out the squares.

Hem the napkins

3   With the wrong side of the fabric facing up, press under a ¼" double-fold hem (see page 34) on two opposite raw edges of the napkins. Stitch the hem in place and press.

4   Repeat step 3 on the remaining opposite raw edges. Trim away any bulkiness that will help you turn under the fabric at the corners.

Dish Towel

Of course you can buy dish towels in all kinds of stores, but it's so easy to make your own. They also make a terrific housewarming or hostess gift. Personally, I don't think you can ever have too many, but if you end up with a surplus, they can be repurposed to make all kinds of other goodies for your home, such as pillows, curtains, aprons, coasters, and more!

Our finished size

20" x 24"

What you'll need

◆ ¾ yard of fabric will make 2 dish towels
◆ 4" strip of ¾"-wide twill tape

Measure and cut the fabric

1   Measure and mark two 22"x 26" rectangles on the wrong side of the fabric. (You can fit two 22"-wide rectangles side by side on 44/45"-wide fabric.) Cut them out.

Pin the hems and twill tape

2   For each dish towel, do the following: With the wrong side of the fabric facing up, press under a ½" double-fold hem on two opposite raw edges. Pin to hold in place, but do not stitch yet.

3   Repeat step 2 on the remaining opposite raw edges.

4   Position the strip of twill tape into one of the corners on the diagonal, inside the folded edge. Trim the edges of the tape on the diagonal for a better fit, and pin in place.

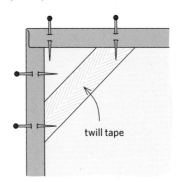

twill tape

Stitch the hems

5   Stitch evenly around all four edges, securing the twill tape in the corner.

EMBELLISHMENTS

Dish towels can be quite decorative. You can easily add rickrack, pom-poms, or ribbon for some extra pizzazz. This is also a terrific chance to try out embroidery or appliqué. Just remember that dish towels are used in the kitchen, where things can get messy, so they'll need to be machine washable.

Tea Cozy

This retro fabric was so terrific, we kept the tea cozy simple to show it off. But if you want to embroider a design or try your hand at appliqué, this is a great project on which to play and experiment. We used a fleece lining to keep the teapot warm without extra layers, but if you choose to use two light-weight fabrics, be sure to add some batting between them for insulation.

Our finished size

8" tall x 10" wide

What you'll need

- ¼ yard of fabric
- ¼ yard of fleece or flannel
- 3" piece of ½" twill tape

Measure your teapot

1   Measure the circumference (distance around), divide by two, and add 2" for ease and seam allowances.

2   Measure from the top center of the teapot down to the table and add 2".

Measure and cut

3   Following your measurements, cut two pieces of exterior fabric and two pieces of the fleece.

4   Select one of the pieces and lay it on a flat surface. Decide which will be the top edge. Measure and mark 3" from each top corner in both directions. Cut off the corners between the marks. Use this piece as a template to cut the same corners out of the other fabric piece and both fleece pieces.

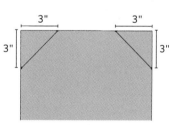

Assemble and stitch the tea cozy

5   With right sides facing, pin one fabric piece to a fleece piece along the bottom edge. Stitch along this edge, then turn the pieces so the

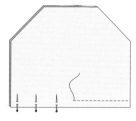

wrong sides are facing and the seam allowance is between the two pieces. Press along the seam line, then edgestitch ¼" from the seam edge. Repeat this process for the remaining fabric and fleece pieces.

6 Pin the two stitched pairs together with the fabric right sides facing. Fold the twill tape in half and tuck it in the center of the top between the center fabrics, aligning raw edges. Stitch along all raw edges.

7 Trim and notch the corner seam allowances and turn the tea cozy right side out. Set the kettle on to boil!

Pick fabrics to match the mood and style of your teacups.

SQUARE TABLECLOTH

Covering up an old table has to be the easiest make-over of them all. It's like magic. A simple tablecloth can change an entire room by adding color, pattern, and texture — and by drawing focus to the table itself. Not only is the transition simple, so is actually making the tablecloth.

First measure the top of your table (width and length). Then measure the desired drop; anywhere from 8" to 12" is pretty standard. Since the tablecloth needs to "drop" on both sides of the width and the length, add twice the drop to those measurements, plus seam allowance for the hem. For example, if your table is 40" x 30" and you want a 12" drop, you would add 24" to each of your measurements, plus 4" for the 1" double-fold hems on either side. So you'd cut your fabric to 68" x 58".

Mark your dimensions on the wrong side of the fabric and cut. Make a double-fold hem on two opposite raw edges, then repeat with the remaining edges.

CHAPTER 8

Party On

WHEN IT'S TIME FOR A PARTY, set aside your table for two and convert a folding table into a glorious buffet. You don't need a party planner to make your soirée a smash. Work with what you've got! You'll be surprised by how easy it is transform your dining room with a few items custom-made for your special occasion. This setup is a tribute to the versatility of fabric. From a rugged roller shade to a flowing table skirt and soft organza bags, the key is picking the right fabric for the function. The table skirt invites creative variations to fit the occasion. You could imagine brightly colored circle shapes for a kid's birthday party or even fringe or appliquéd flowers for a special theme party.

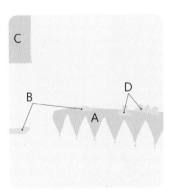

A. *Beaded Table Skirt*

B. *Lined Cocktail Napkins*

C. *Roller Shade*

D. *Goodie Bags*

Beaded Table Skirt

This table "miniskirt" is just the ticket for transforming a folding table into party central. Choose materials that work for your event and occasion, and make table skirts for use indoors or out — for picnics, birthday parties, or a cocktail party bar. We added beads to the ends and used some extras to make beaded charms for the glasses. If you don't have beads, you can stitch buttons on the ends instead!

Our finished size

top panel 21" x 49"; side triangles 9" long

What you'll need

- 1½ yards of 54"-wide fabric for the top panel, depending on the size of your table
- 1½ to 3 yards of 54"-wide fabric for the side panels, depending on the size of your table
- 12 sets of beads and jewelry headpins, or enough for each triangle point
- Needle-nose pliers

Measure your table and cut the fabric

1 Measure your tabletop (our table was 20" x 48"). Add 2" for seam allowance and overhang.

2 On the wrong side of the top panel fabric, draw a rectangle across the fabric to your dimensions. Cut out the fabric.

3 Use the top panel as a template to cut two rectangles the same size from the side panel fabric.

Make the top panel

4 Make a ¼" double-fold hem (see page 34) on the short ends of the top panel. Set aside.

Make the side triangles

5 Place one of the side panels onto the table with the right side facing up. Fold in half along its length, then fold again into thirds. From the top down, fold in half one more time.

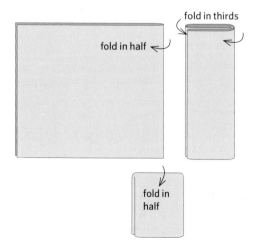

fold in thirds

fold in half

fold in half

6   Mark 2" down from the top folded edge on both
    sides. Find and mark the center of the bottom
    edge, and draw lines from there to each side mark.

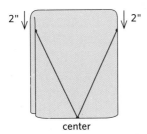

7   Cut along the lines to remove the bottom corners.
    Open up the fabric to reveal a double layer of six
    triangles. Cut along the top fold to separate into
    two strips.

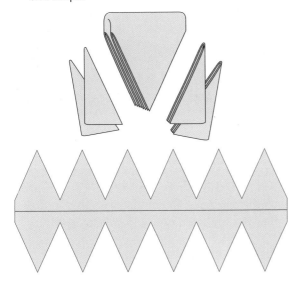

8   Repeat steps 5–7 with the remaining side panel
    rectangle to make two more strips of triangles.

Assemble and stitch the pieces

9   With right sides facing, pin two strips of triangles
    together. Stitch the sides and around the triangle
    points as shown, leaving the top edge open. Trim
    the points and clip the inside corners of all the tri-
    angles. Repeat with the remaining triangle strips.

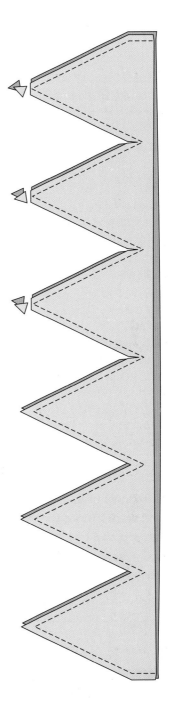

STEP 9

10 Turn both triangle strips right side out and press. Edgestitch ¼" around the triangle points.

11 With right sides together, pin one of the triangle strips to one long side of the top panel, aligning raw edges. Stitch, and then press the seam allowance toward the center. Attach the second triangle strip on the other side.

Embellish the skirt

12 Thread the beads onto the headpins in whatever design you like (we used one large colored bead with two smaller beads on both sides). Use pliers to bend the top of each headpin into a loop. Hand-sew each looped end onto a triangle point.

Lined Cocktail Napkins

These classy little cocktail napkins are fun and fresh. We chose a crisp white lining. You can line yours with a contrasting or complementary print instead. Because cocktail napkins are a little bit smaller than dinner napkins, you can use scraps or large swatches. And if you make them reversible, you can play with the look of the table . . . instead of playing with your food!

Our finished size

11" square

What you'll need

- 12" fabric squares, or ⅓ yard of 44–45"-wide fabric will make 3 napkin fronts
- 12" fabric squares, or ⅓ yard for the lining

Measure and cut the fabric

1 On the wrong side of the fabric, measure and mark two 12" squares (front and lining) for each napkin you plan to make. Or measure and cut one square, then use it as a template to cut the others.

Stitch the napkins

2 With right sides facing, pin each front piece to a lining piece. Stitch on all sides, leaving a 4" opening along one side. Clip the corners (see page 32).

3 Turn each napkin right side out and push out the corners with a point turner. Tuck the seam allowances neatly inside the openings and press. Slipstitch each opening closed, or edgestitch ⅛" from the edge all the way around each napkin.

Roller Shade

We've all used those plain white vinyl roller shades at one time or another. Sure, they do the trick for privacy, and keep it dark in the morning so we can catch a little extra shut-eye. But they really don't do a whole lot for a room, do they? And they aren't terribly festive. Here's a simple redo of the roller shade that's quick and easy. Match your party décor the day before the event — you can even do the whole thing without sewing a stitch!

Our finished size

24" wide x 80" long

What you'll need

- 1 roller shade that fits the desired window
- Fabric to replace the vinyl (ours uses 2¼ yards)
- Liquid fray preventer
- Staple gun and staples

Remove the vinyl

1 Remove the vinyl shade from the barrel. Be sure to mark the direction of the hang to avoid confusion later. Also remove the wooden or plastic slat at the bottom of the vinyl shade. Set the barrel and slat aside.

Prepare and cut the fabric

2 Lay the vinyl on the wrong side of the fabric as a template, marking the outline with a straightedge or metal yardstick and a tailor's pencil adding 1½" at bottom for hem. Remove the vinyl. Do not cut out yet.

   NOTE: *Since the sides will not be hemmed, make sure the selvage is not included within the outline.*

3 Apply liquid fray preventer along the entire length of the cutout lines. Allow it to dry.

4 Using a rotary cutter, ruler, and mat, carefully cut out the fabric.

Hem the bottom edge

5 Stitch a double-fold hem at the bottom edge that is wide enough to contain the slat. Ours was pressed under ¼" and then 1", but check the old vinyl shade and measure your slat. Adjust the hem accordingly.

Assemble the shade

6 Insert the dowel or slat into the bottom hem.

7 Staple the top edge to the barrel, making sure to follow the direction of the hang you marked earlier. Hang your roller shade.

Goodie Bags

These sweet sacks can be teeny tiny or larger, depending on what kind of goodies you'll be doling out. It's fun to offer favors — why leave them only to the kids? Grownups like goodie bags, too! Of course, you can choose fabrics that suit any occasion, and the bag itself is a gift that can be reused or regifted.

Our finished size

5" x 8"

What you'll need

- Two 7" x 13" fabric scraps (or your preferred size)
- 1¼ yards of ¼" ribbon for ties

FABRIC NOTE

The fabric you use will affect how you make the casing. We used organza, a transparent fabric that doesn't have a distinct right side/wrong side, so we turned our casing to the outside and let the hemmed edge show. If your fabric has an obvious wrong side, turn your casing to the inside.

Even up the raw edges

1 Use a rotary cutter, ruler, and mat to even up the edges of the fabric scraps to 6" x 12".

Make the casing

2 For each fabric piece, press under the top edge 1", then press under another 2½". Edgestitch along the bottom fold, then stitch again ½" above the first stitch line. This should catch the 1" folded edge beneath.

Stitch the sides

3 With right sides facing, pin together the two pieces. Starting at the top edge, backstitch to the casing, then backstitch again. Skip over the casing, backstitch on the other side, then stitch around to the casing on the other side and backstitch. Skip over the casing, backstitch, then stitch to the top edge and backstitch.

4 Trim the corners. Finish the raw edges above the casing with a zigzag stitch or serger. Depending on the fabric you use, you may need to clip the seam allowance above the casing to help when threading the ribbon. Leave the bag wrong side out.

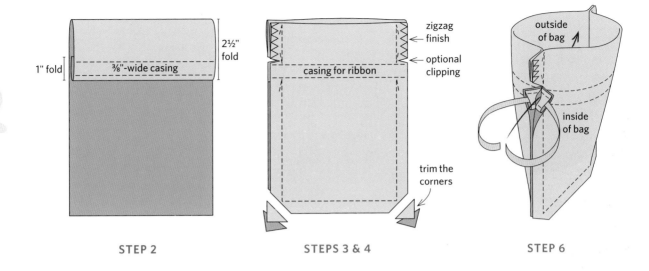

| STEP 2 | STEPS 3 & 4 | STEP 6 |

Insert the drawstring

5 Fold the ribbon in half along its length and cut to make two pieces.

RIBBON NOTE

If making a larger or smaller bag, measure the width of your bag, triple that measurement, and cut each ribbon to that length.

6 Use a safety pin to thread one ribbon into the casing. Instead of coming out the opposite side, turn the end around and thread it through the casing on the opposite side of the bag back to the beginning. Thread both ends through the casing hole in the seam (as shown) to push the ribbon ends to the right side. Thread the remaining ribbon through the casings in the same way, but starting on the opposite side of the bag.

7 Turn the bag right side out. Match up the ribbon ends on both sides of the bag and knot them together. Pull on both ribbons at the same time to gather the bag.

CHAPTER 9

A Swell Affair

PARTIES CAN BE DAUNTING, but don't let a plain dining room stop you from inviting a crowd to your table. Your own style and a little creative vision will dress up any room from dull to dazzling. Personal touches are the most inviting. For this table setting, we worked with just three fairly neutral fabrics to achieve a pleasing, unified look that has a classic feel to it. These basic designs are wonderfully functional as well as pretty and quite versatile. So, find the fabric combination that resonates most with your style, occasion, or the season and start stitching! Your guests won't know what to admire the most: your handiwork, your cooking, or your relaxed smile as you welcome them inside.

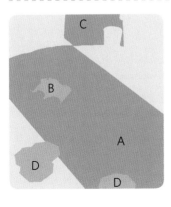

A. *Table Runner*

B. *Chalkboard Napkin Rings or Place Cards*

C. *Classic Apron*

D. *M'octagonal Coasters*

Table Runner

No matter what shape your table is, a simple runner is just the ticket. It livens up the room beautifully and draws attention to the horizontal line of the table. Plus, by using a runner and not a tablecloth, we've created the opportunity to make a few more nifty projects to deck out the table for our dinner party scene.

Our finished size

17" x 60"

What you'll need

♦ 1¾ yard of each fabric used (you will have fabric left over for another project)

REVERSIBLE OPTION

This table runner can be reversible, doubling your makeover options. If you like, choose two different fabrics for the back and make it in the same way as the front, with two contrasting edges. Your call! When mixing and matching fabrics, check care instructions to make sure they are a suitable match.

Measure and cut

1 Measure your table to decide the width of your table runner. Leave about 10" of open space on each side of the table for place settings. For the length, make it short enough so two additional place settings will fit at the heads of the table, or make it longer and let it hang over the short ends of the table. Add 1" to both the width and length measurements for seam allowances.

2 Using scissors and a yardstick, or a rotary cutter and cutting mat, cut a piece of fabric to this size. This piece will be the back of the table runner. (Our back piece was 18" x 61".)

3 For the top, cut two side strips that are 3½" wide x the length measurement. Lay these two strips on top of the back piece. Measure the space between the strips and add 1" to include two seam allowances. Cut the center piece to that measurement x the length. (Our side strips were 3½" x 61"; our center piece was 13" x 61".)

Stitch the front pieces

4   Lay the center front piece on a flat surface, right side up. With right sides facing, pin the long strips on either side of the center piece. Stitch a ½" seam on both sides and press seams open.

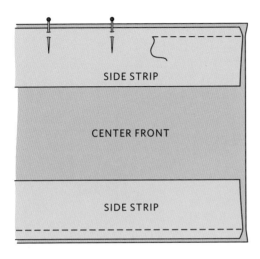

SIDE STRIP

CENTER FRONT

SIDE STRIP

Stitch front and back together

5   The front and the back should now be the same size. Pin them with right sides facing and stitch on all sides, leaving a 3" opening on one end for turning.

6   Trim the corners, turn the runner right side out, and press. Slipstitch the opening closed.

VARIATIONS

Runners can be made to fit any table size or surface and used in just about any room of the house — in the dining room or kitchen, on a buffet, sideboard, end tables, you name it. A piece of vintage linen or a flea market hankie can add just the right touch to your powder room or bedside table. Drape a runner over a solid or complementary tablecloth for a softer look. You can even gussy up your coffee table during the big game!

Chalkboard Napkin Rings or Place Cards

This cool project is a twofer. You can wrap the chalkboard oilcloth pieces around the napkins and tie them up for a pretty picture, or lay them flat to use as place cards. These reusable cards are perfect for family gatherings or big dinner parties.

Our finished size

3" x 6½"

What you'll need

- ♦ ¼ yard of chalkboard oilcloth fabric (will make 10 napkin rings)
- ♦ ½ yard of ½" black twill tape per napkin ring
- ♦ Chalk pencil for writing names

Measure and cut the fabric

1 On the back of the oilcloth, measure and mark a 4" x 7½" strip for each napkin ring. Use shears or a rotary cutter, ruler, and mat to cut out the strips.

Hem the edges

2 Make a ½" single-fold hem on the long sides of the strips, using a zigzag stitch. Do the same on the two short ends, trimming away extra bulk to help you stitch around the corner.

Cut the ties

3 To use as napkin rings, wrap each strip around a napkin and tie with ribbon. To use as place cards, write a name on each strip with chalk. Wipe names off with a damp cloth to reuse.

Classic Apron

Don't have a thing to wear? Don't be silly! Servers all over the world don aprons just like this one. The classic look is tailored and comfortable and the style couldn't be easier to wear. When working in the kitchen or serving your guests, this apron feels professional and elegant, just like working in a five-star restaurant. Bon appétit!

Our finished size

30" high x 30" wide (one size fits most)

What you'll need

- 1 yard of fabric for the apron
- ¼ yard or 9" x 14" scrap of fabric for pocket panel (matching or complementary)
- 2 yards of 1"-wide twill tape for belt (or enough to wrap around your waist twice and tie)

Measure and cut

1   On the wrong side of the fabric, measure, mark, and cut a 34" x 36" rectangle for the body of the apron.

2   Cut a 9" x 14" rectangle for the pocket panel.

Hem the edges

3   For the apron body:
- Press under a 1" double-fold hem (see page 34) on the left and right edges of the apron, then stitch.
- On the bottom raw edge, press and stitch a 2" double-fold hem.
- Leave the top edge raw for now.

4   For the pocket panel:
- Press under and stitch a ¼" double-fold hem on the left and right edges.
- Press under and stitch a ¼" double-fold hem on the bottom edge.

- Along the top edge, press under and stitch a ½" double-fold hem.

Attach the pocket panel

5   Fold the apron in half lengthwise and press the center fold. Do the same with the pocket panel. Open up both pieces. Matching up the center folds, pin the pocket panel 6¾" from the top edge of the apron.

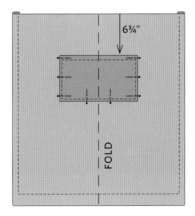

6   Stitch down one side of the pocket, across the bottom, and up the other side, backstitching at both ends. Stitch down the pressed center line, backstitching at both ends, to make two pockets.

Attach the belt

7   Press under and stitch a 1" double-fold hem on the top edge of the apron.

8   Press under the short ends of the twill tape ½" and stitch in place. Fold the tape in half lengthwise and mark the center fold with a pin.

9   With the right side facing up, position the twill tape on the top edge of the apron, lining up the center point with the center fold and the top edge of the tape with the top edge of the apron. Pin the belt in place, then edgestitch along the top and bottom edges.

10 To reinforce the belt, add a box stitch (see page 31) to the twill tape on both side edges of the apron.

Change the length, change the fabric, and a classic becomes trendy.

M'octagonal Coasters

It's easy to remember to use coasters when they're fun to look at. We used coordinating solid fabric on the bottom of our coasters, to make them reversible. But you can also use felt as the bottom fabric, which adds a nice, nonslip touch.

Finished size

4" across

What you'll need

 ◆ 5" square of heavy paper or card stock for making a template
 ◆ Two 5" fabric squares per coaster (2 fat quarters of different fabrics will make 12 coasters)
 ◆ ⅓ yard of fusible interfacing

Make a template

1   Make sure your template paper is 5" square, then make a mark 1½" from each corner. Connect the lines and cut off the corners to make an octagon.

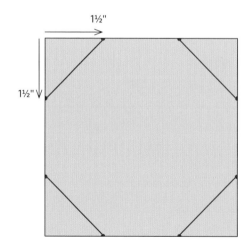

Fuse on interfacing

2 Decide which of your fabrics to interface, and fuse the interfacing to the wrong side, following manufacturer's directions.

Cut and fold the fabric

3 Use your template to trace octagons onto the wrong side of both fabrics. Cut them out.

4 Press under opposite edges ½" as shown, then press under the remaining raw edges ½".

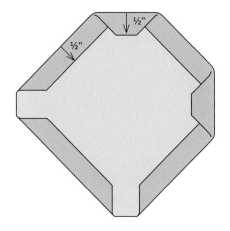

Stitch the coasters

5 Match up top and bottom fabrics with wrong sides together. Pin and then edgestitch ⅛" from the edge on all sides. Stitch a second row ⅛" inside the first stitch line. Iced tea, anyone?

THE SHAPE OF THINGS

We call these "M'octagonal" because you probably won't end up with exact octagons. Personally, I don't think it matters. This isn't about making perfect shapes, but making fun coasters! Play up the geometry by selecting fabric designs with distinctive shape imagery.

A Room that Grows Up (Along with the Kids)

As children grow, so do their needs — and their burgeoning personalities! Almost nowhere in the house requires a makeover as often as a child's room. What you plan for a newborn won't work when the kid is eight. A baby might move out of the nursery and into an older sibling's room at some point, or kids who share a room now might get their own spaces down the road. And, of course, each child will have periods of new "favorites" over time. This is an excellent opportunity to see just how far these little mini-makeovers can go. In this chapter, we'll look at three kid spaces: one for a baby, one for a young child, and one for an older child about to hit the teens. The idea is to show you how a few projects can transform a space entirely.

Tween Spirit

Baby Mine

Pee Wee Playhouse

CHAPTER 10

Baby Mine

BOY OR GIRL, TWINS OR SEXTUPLETS, YOU'LL WANT IT ALL FOR YOUR NEWBIES. But bringing up Baby doesn't require going overboard in the décor department. It means creating a very special place for the most magical additions to the home. Harmonious colors and textures are the key ingredients for a soothing and uplifting nursery. Many of these projects offer great ways for using up fabric scraps and for incorporating bits of fabric that have special family memories associated with them. Just imagine your little one seeing and feeling these things for the very first time, and have fun pulling the elements together. And by the way, congratulations!

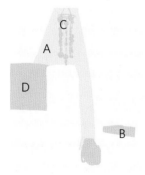

A. *Tulle Canopy*

B. *Box Cushion*

C. *Felt Mobile*

D. *Improv Appliqué Blankie*

Tulle Canopy

There's nothin' like a nest to keep your little egg warm and cozy. This soft, breezy canopy creates a shelter, while still letting Baby see the world all around. Don't feel like hemming tulle today? Not a problem. This canopy can be made as a no-sew project, too — just hang lightweight curtains, drapes, or even a fabric shower curtain on the embroidery hoop instead.

Our finished size

each panel is 54" x 83"

What you'll need

- 5 yards of 54"-wide tulle
- One 10" embroidery hoop (the outer ring only)
- ¾ yard of ½" ribbon
- Fabric scraps
- 1 O-ring
- 1 ceiling hook

Cut the fabric

1 Fold the tulle in half and cut along the fold, creating two 54" x 90" panels.

Stitch the panels

2 Hem the edges of both panels as follows:
  - Stitch ½" double-fold hems (see page 34) on both sides.
  - On the top and bottom edges, press under 3½". Stitch ½" from the raw edge.

Stitch the ribbon hanger

3 Fold the ribbon in half and cut into two strips of equal length. Thread one end of each strip through the O-ring. Fold under ¼", then ½", and stitch just outside the O-ring.

TULLE TIPS

Tulle is a netted fabric with a soft, floating appearance. While it looks difficult to sew on, it is really quite simple. It's helpful, however, to stabilize your seam while you're sewing it. One easy way to do this is to place a 1"-wide strip of tissue paper on the underside of the tulle and run your sewing machine stitching over all layers. Once your seam is completed, carefully pull the tissue paper layer off.

Assemble on the hoop

4 Loosen the clamp on the embroidery hoop, open it, and slide the panels on to it, one at a time.

5 In between the two panels, position the raw ends of the ribbons. Fold them under ¼", then ½", and stitch as you did with the O-ring.

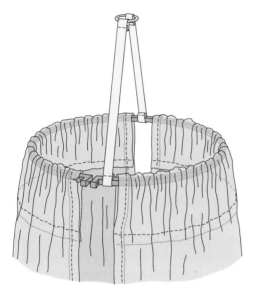

Hang the canopy

6 Screw a hook into the ceiling over the child's bed and hang the O-ring from the hook. Drape the ends of the tulle on the sides of the baby's crib or cradle.

Box Cushion

In a baby nursery, cushions are a must-have for feeding, reading, snuggling, and rocking. If you make your own, any chair can be styled to fit to the nursery décor. Box cushions can also be used as floor cushions or on benches, window seats, or patio furniture. We painted our wicker chair to keep the furniture crisp white all around, but natural wicker looks just as nice.

Our finished size
19½" x 19½" x 3"

What you'll need

- 1 foam cushion, 19" x 19" x 3" or desired size to fit a chair
- 1 yard of fabric (see step 1 measurements)
- One 22" zipper
- ½"-wide double-stick fusible web tape

1 If you're making a cushion the same size as ours, skip to step 2. If using your own size, you'll need the following measurements:

   ◆ For the top and bottom pieces, measure the length and width of the foam, then add 1" to each measurement for seam allowance.

   ◆ For side piece A, measure the depth of the foam and add 1". Then measure all the way around the sides, divide by two, and add 1".

   ◆ For side piece B (the zipper section), measure the depth of the foam, divide by two, and add 1". The length will be the same as the other side piece.

Measure and cut the fabric

2 Measure and cut the fabric, using your measurements or the ones provided:

   ◆ 2 squares for the top and bottom (20½")
   ◆ 1 of side piece A (4" x 40")
   ◆ 2 of side piece B (2½" x 40")

Install the zipper

3 Install the zipper into the side B pieces, using fusible tape (see page 35).

UNZIPPED

If you don't want the zipper, you can cut two of side A instead of one and use it to replace the zipper strip. When stitching the top (step 6), leave most of one side open, for turning the cover and inserting the foam cushion. Slipstitch the opening closed.

Stitch the sides

4 Side pieces A and B should now be the same width and length. With right sides facing, pin the two strips together at the short ends and stitch them together to form a continuous loop. Press seams open.

Assemble the cover

5 With right sides facing, pin the side strip to the bottom square, positioning the zipper and seams as shown. You want the zipper to turn the corner on both ends of one side. The seam between A and B pieces will be halfway between the corners on opposite sides.

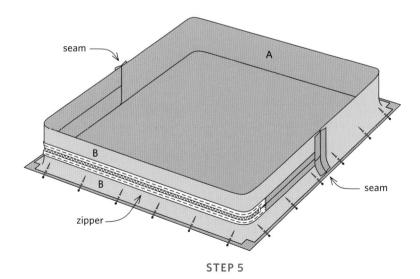

seam

A

seam

B

B

zipper

STEP 5

6   As you pin, you will need to make a small (less than ½") clip at each corner of the side panel to ease it around the corners. Be careful not to cut too far. With the side facing you, stitch all the way around the cushion.

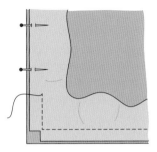

7   Unzip the zipper partway. With right sides facing, pin the sides to the top square of the cushion in the same way as the bottom and sew (steps 5 and 6).

8   Trim corners, trim seam allowance as needed, and press seams open. Pull the cover right side out through the zipper opening.

Insert the foam

9   Open the zipper all the way and insert the foam. Close the zipper.

Felt Mobile

For this cheerful mobile we used bright solid-colored felt to complement the fabrics in the room. Another option is to cut circles out of a print fabric and stitch them to the back of the felt, or use multiple fabrics in multiple colors. Try tracing cookie cutters onto the felt instead of circles and string up rows of stars, hearts, letters, or animals. Wherever you hang the mobile, be sure the strands are securely attached to the hoop, and they are out of baby's reach.

Our finished size

10" hoop; longest strand is 40"

What you'll need

- 26 felt circles, in varying sizes
- Invisible nylon thread
- Inner ring of a 10" embroidery hoop
- 2½ yards of ½" ribbon
- One 1" O-ring
- 1 ceiling hook

SAFETY FIRST

When making your mobile, be sure the strands and circles are attached securely. Remember that anything in your baby's room, especially in, near, or over the bed or crib, can pose a potential safety risk. Please use caution — and your head — when making this or anything else for your baby and children.

be any length; for the others, make two pairs that are the same length, for balance. Keep in mind that the first circle you sew will be at the bottom of the strand, as you'll be sewing from the bottom up to the top circle.

3 Using invisible thread, stitch down the middle of the first (bottom) felt circle. Backstitch at the end and add on the next circle. Backstitch on that circle as well, then stitch down the middle. Keep adding circles in the same way to complete the strand. Leave the thread long at the end, so you can tie the strand to the embroidery hoop. Repeat for the other four strands.

TIP

Use a slightly longer stitch and the small-hole throat plate on your machine to keep the felt from feeding down into the machine and getting jammed.

Make the hanger

4 Fold the ribbon in half twice, and cut into four strips of equal length. Thread one end of each strip through the O-ring. Fold under ¼", then ½", and stitch just outside the O-ring.

5 Lay the O-ring on a table with the four ribbons stretching out like spokes on a wheel. Lay the hoop on top, with the O-ring in the center. Fold each ribbon over the hoop and hand-sew the two sides of each ribbon together around the hoop, leaving the long ends free. Gather the free ends of the ribbon together, fold them over twice, and stitch to form a loop for hanging.

Measure and cut the felt

1 Cut out felt circles in various sizes. Ours are 1½", 2", and 3½".

Stitch the circles into strands

2 Lay out five lines of circles on a flat surface, alternating sizes as often as you like until you reach your desired length. The center strand can

Attach the strands

6   From the bottom of the hoop, use a needle to hand-sew each strand securely to each ribbon on the hoop. Attach the strands of equal length opposite each other on the hoop. For the central strand, bridge the gap by hand-sewing it to two ribbons on opposite sides of the O-ring.

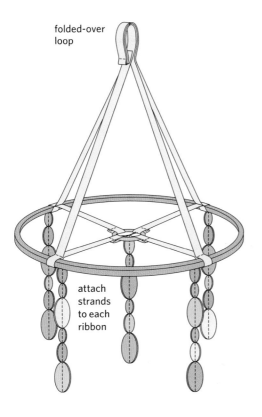

folded-over loop

attach strands to each ribbon

Hang the mobile

7   Screw a hook into the ceiling and hang the loop from the hook.

Improv Appliqué Blankie

A blankie like this is a cinch to make, and a wonderful way to create memories for your little one. Use any kind of fabric scraps: an older sibling's PJs, your granddad's neckties, or your favorite high school T-shirts. The scraps don't have to be uniform, either. Just piece them together any way you like and . . . improvise! We used a soft cotton tea towel for the backing and cut the fleece front to fit.

Our finished size
29" x 32"

What you'll need

- 1 yard of no-pill fleece
- 1 tea towel or other cotton fabric for backing, 30" x 34"
- Fabric scraps

Measure and cut the fabric

1 If using a tea towel, lay it on the fleece and cut the fleece to the same size. Or cut the fleece and other cotton fabric to the same desired size, using a rotary cutter, ruler, and mat.

2 Cut out whatever shapes you like from fabric scraps. We cut circles, which are simple to trace by using small plates, saucers, or plastic lids as templates.

Plan and appliqué your design

3 Lay the fleece side of the blankie on a flat surface. Move the cutout pieces around on the fleece until you are satisfied with the layout. Use safety pins to hold each piece in place.

4 Using a zigzag or satin stitch, stitch each fabric shape to the fleece. It helps to start with the fabrics at the center and work your way outward.

Stitch the blankie edges

5 With right sides together, pin the appliquéd fleece and backing along the raw edges. Stitch around the perimeter, leaving a 6" opening.

6 Trim excess seam allowance, taking care not to cut the edges of the opening too closely. Trim the corners. Turn the quilt right side out, press, and slipstitch the opening closed.

VARIATION

Finish the edges of the blanket by adding bias binding, hand-sewing a blanket stitch shown below, or making a funky edge with a machine zigzag or satin stitch. It's all about improvisation, so try any style that suits you!

MAKE A BAG TO FIT THE ROOM

I'm a big believer in having many bags, each with the right structure and features to fit the purpose. My first book, *Sew What! Bags*, features simple plans for making a variety of totes and carryalls designed to fit the function. A coordinating diaper bag is a perfect complement to your new nursery. There are four basic parts to this bag: front, back, bottom, and two sides (see diagram). You can add inside pockets, as desired, and finish it off with straps.

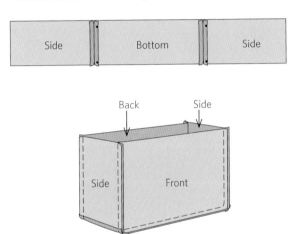

CHAPTER 11

Pee Wee Playhouse

DECORATING FOR SMALL CHILDREN CAN MAKE YOU LAUGH — or make you nuts! Between their latest favorite color and their newest imaginary friend, you never know what they might like today. But there is a secret, and it's called make-believe. Even the littlest change in a pee wee's room can make the world spin in a new direction. Bedecked with a bit of fabric, the bedroom becomes the perfect backdrop for magical adventures and playful dreaming. See how we kept the same cozy feeling as the nursery (page 103), but changed the look entirely? Enjoy whipping up new projects during this amazing time and encourage your child to help make them!

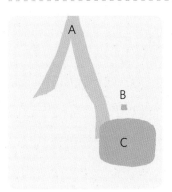

A. *Bedtime Backdrop*

B. *Night-Light Lamp Shade Cover*

C. *Marshmallow Cushion*

Switch Plate Cover
(shown on pages 118 and 119)

Bedtime Backdrop

When little ones reach their preschool years, their creativity soars. Nurture their dreams by giving them a fabulous place to experience them. It's so easy to hang fabric that you can change the room's décor any time for a change of scenery. If you don't want to splurge on brand-new fabric, use drapes or bedsheets. For a quicker switch, skip the lining and just hang up the fabric.

Our finished size

39" x 80"

What you'll need

- 4½ yards of fabric (adjust as needed)
- 4½ yards of complementary or white fabric for the lining (adjust as needed)
- 1 plant hanger (as long as possible, 12" to 18")

SAFETY TIP

Make sure the hanger is high enough to protect your child's head and to deter unwanted climbing.

Cut the fabric

1 Decide how high you'd like the canopy to hang and measure down to the floor. It's best to do this in the room where the backdrop will hang; allow enough drape for around the bed. Double the measurement to allow for two panels, and add 2" to the length for seam allowances.

2 The easiest way to cut the fabric is to fold it in half lengthwise and cut along the fold. We cut ours to 40" wide, but you might want to use the full width of the fabric. Cut both the outer fabric and the lining.

Stitch the sides

3 With right sides facing, pin together one outer panel and one lining on all sides. Stitch all the way around, leaving a 7" to 10" opening at the top. Do the same with the remaining panel and lining.

4 For both panels, clip the corners (see page 32) and trim seam allowances. Turn the panels right side out, tuck in the seam allowance at the opening, and press. Do not stitch the opening yet.

Make the casing

5 With the outer fabrics facing, pin the two panels together along the top edge, keeping the seam allowances tucked inside. Stitch a ¼" seam.

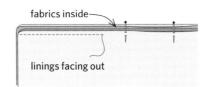

fabrics inside

linings facing out

6 Press the seam open, then fold the panels along the seam with the seam allowance and linings inside. Pin the layers together, measure 3" or 4" down from the seam, and draw a line with fabric marker or chalk. Stitch along the line to make the casing, backstitching at the ends.

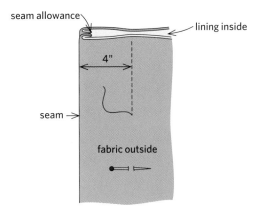

seam allowance

lining inside

4"

seam →

fabric outside

Hang the backdrop

7 Attach the plant hanger to the wall, following manufacturer's instructions. Thread the fabric onto hanger and arrange the drape. Stand back and watch the fun begin!

ALL IN THE FAMILY

Invite your children to help map out their room make-overs. If they are interested, find ways to let them "help" with the painting and sewing. Learning to make choices and to think about their needs, while exploring their own sense of style, is priceless. Some basic decorating skills will help your kids later when moving away to school or into their own home someday. For now, though, just enjoy the process and encourage your children to participate!

Night-Light Lamp Shade Cover

You never know — there might be ghosts, goblins, or monsters just waiting to come out after dark. Never fear, the night-light is here! But some night-lights are just plain better than others. This one has a funky half-shade that I couldn't resist making over. You can easily adapt these instructions for a small bedside lamp shade.

Our finished size

3¼" high x 6½" at the base

What you'll need

- 1 night-light with half-shade
- Fabric scrap large enough to cover the shade
- Spray adhesive (see Safety First! on page 28)
- ½ yard of extra-wide double-fold bias tape
- Hot glue gun and glue sticks
- Glitter
- Fabric glue or white glue

Make a template

1   Place the lamp shade onto a sheet of paper. Roll the shade slowly and trace the top and bottom edges as you go. Mark the end points and draw lines to connect the top and bottom. (If you are covering a whole shade, begin and end at the lamp shade seam.)

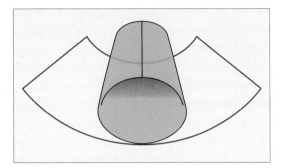

Cut the fabric

2   Cut out the template and place it on the wrong side of your fabric. Cut out the fabric and check to make sure it's a good fit.

FABRIC NOTE

If you will be adding bias tape to the top and bottom edges, like we did, cut the fabric exactly the same size as your template. If you want to skip the trim and just wrap the edges of the fabric over the top and bottom edges of the lamp shade, you'll need to add a 1" seam allowance.

Cover the lamp shade

3   Apply spray adhesive to the wrong side of the fabric, following manufacturer's directions, and wrap it around the existing shade. (If you are covering a whole shade, fold under the overlapping edge ¼" and use hot glue at the seam, smoothing out the glue so it doesn't create a bump.)

Embellish as desired

4   We attached bias tape to the top and bottom edges of our lamp shade, but you can use ribbon, fringe, or cording. Affix with hot glue, lining up the ends of the trim with the edges of the shade cover and using fray preventer on the ends if needed. Just for fun, we stuck on some glitter with glue. For inspiration, look to lamp shades on pages 75 and 124. All can be made the same way!

VARIATIONS

These mini lamp shades are a fun way to play with notions and trims.

Pom-poms complement this lively print.

Combine gold trim and a classy print for a more formal look.

Marshmallow Cushion

On the floor, on the grass, in the sand . . . no matter where they go, little ones love to be low to the ground. A big, soft, fluffy "marshmallow" pillow is the perfect spot for some quiet time, reading a book, gazing at the moon through the window, or sharing stories with a good friend.

Our finished size

27" circle

What you'll need

- ⅞ yard of muslin (for lining the top)
- ⅞ yard of 2 complementary fabrics (for top and bottom)
- ½ yard of fabric (for side panel)
- ½"-wide double-stick fusible web tape
- One 14" zipper
- A few bags of recycled packing material (see step 7)

FABRIC NOTE

If you are using heavier fabric, such as canvas or home decorator or upholstery weight, you may not need the muslin lining. Remember to cut notches into the side when you stitch it to the top and bottom circles.

Measure and cut the fabric

1   On the wrong side of the muslin, measure, mark, and cut a 28" circle (see Going in Circles on page 118). Use the circle as a template to cut two from the large fabric pieces.

2   For the side panel, cut a 16" rectangle x the width of the fabric. To make it easier to install the zipper, fold the rectangle in half lengthwise and cut along the fold to make two 16" x 22" rectangles.

Install the zipper

3   Install the zipper into the short ends of the side pieces, using fusible tape (see page 35). Then stitch the opposite short ends to make a continuous loop. Staystitch both edges.

Stitch the parts together

4   Baste the muslin circle to the wrong side of the top circle fabric.

5   With right sides together, pin the side panel to the bottom circle. Clip as needed to fit the strip to the circle, then stitch.

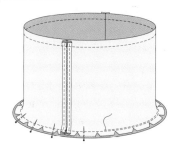

6   Unzip the zipper. With right sides together, pin the side panel to the top circle, clipping the strip as needed, and stitch. Turn the cushion right side out through the zipper opening.

Stuff the cushion

7   Stuff the cushion with anything soft to puff up the marshmallow, such as recycled packing material, fabric scraps, or recycled plastic bags.

GOING IN CIRCLES

Here's how to cut a big circle from fabric:

- For this project, start with a 30" square of fabric.
- Fold the fabric in half, then fold it in half again to make a smaller 15" square.
- Using a yardstick, measure 14" from the inside circle and trace a curved edge by moving the tape measure from the point of the square like a compass.
- Cut out the curve and open up the fabric. You should have a 28" circle.

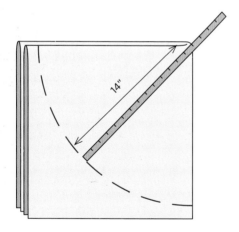

Switch Plate Cover

Kids love decorative details and this is a makeover project that your child can take part in. We covered this switch plate cover with fabric, but you can also use wallpaper, wrapping paper, pages from a vintage book, or your own drawings.

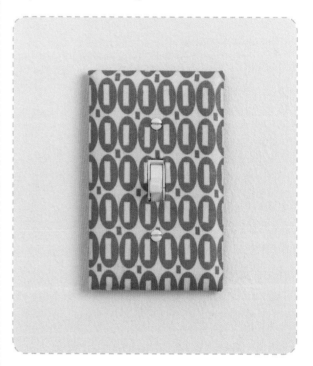

Our finished size

3¼" x 5"

What you'll need

- 1 switch plate
- Fabric scrap bigger than the switch plate
- Utility knife
- Decoupage medium
- Small paintbrush or foam brush
- Masking tape

Trace the switch plate

1 Trace the switch plate onto the wrong side of the fabric. Trace the rectangular opening for the switch and draw an X in the middle of it. Draw another rectangle ½" larger than the switch plate tracing.

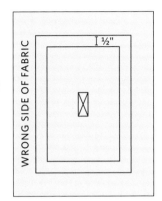

Cut out the fabric

2 Following your markings, cut out the fabric. Carefully cut the X so you have four triangular flaps, taking care not to cut outside the small rectangle.

Apply decoupage medium

3 Lay the fabric on a flat protected surface with the wrong side facing up. Brush the decoupage medium onto the front of the plate and turn it over onto the fabric, centering it within the ½" margin on all sides.

4 Brush the medium onto the edges of the plate and smooth the fabric around the outside edges and inside the switch opening. Allow to dry completely.

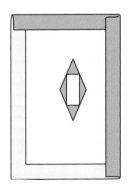

5 Once dry, dab decoupage medium onto the fabric edges on the wrong side of the plate, to paste them securely. Allow to dry.

6 Flip the covered plate over and apply one or two coats of medium over the fabric side of the plate. For a smoother finish, lightly sand between layers.

7 From the front of the plate, locate the screw holes and make a tiny cut into each one with a utility knife or scissors. Screw the plate to the light switch.

Even electrical outlets are an opportunity to add a makeover detail to a freshly painted wall.

CHAPTER 12

Smells Like Tween Spirit

THIRD TIME AROUND, WE'VE TAKEN THE SAME ROOM and completely changed the vibe with just a few sewn projects. Sassy and spunky, or mopey and punky, your tween most definitely has something to say. From clothes to music, to shoes and more, these kids want more than ever to make everything their own. This is the perfect time to teach them to sew or paint or just to pitch in. Plan out the space together and make changes that let your tweens express their own ideas. Selecting the fabrics alone is a great experience for a tween seeking to define his or her personal style. You might be surprised how much work kids will do on their own when they're encouraged to make some choices for themselves.

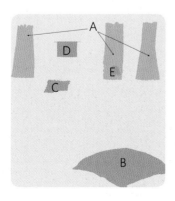

A. *Carefree Curtains*

B. *Ravoli Floor Pillow*

C. *Pom-Pom Pillow*

D. *Hanging Caddy*

E. *Pom-Pom Lamp Shade*
    (see box on page 124)

Carefree Curtains

Curtains can be long and dramatic, light and carefree, or short and sweet. Pair them with a roller shade or blinds to maximize versatility — or simply hang them on their own. You can even hang a single panel, made from sheer fabric, to let the sun shine through.

Our finished size

40" x 60"

What you'll need

- ◆ Curtain rod
- ◆ 1¾ yard of fabric per panel, depending on the size of your windows (see Take Note below)
- ◆ 12 curtain ring clips (optional)
- ◆ 1 yard of ribbon or cording for each tie (optional)

Measure your window

1 Hang your rod in the window and measure from the rod to the windowsill. Also measure the width of the window. Add 4" to the width measurement and 7½" to the length.

TAKE NOTE

Before you measure your window, consider some of these options for length:

- ◆ From the rod to the windowsill (the horizontal board the window closes against)
- ◆ From the rod to the bottom of the window apron or skirt (the board flat against the wall below the sill)
- ◆ From the rod to the floor
- ◆ For an even dreamier effect, cut the curtains about a foot longer than floor length and let the fabric form a "puddle" on the floor.

Measure and cut the fabric

2 On the wrong side of the fabric, use your measurements to mark two panels for the window. You will be making each panel the full width of the window, so they will gather nicely. (In our case, we just used the full width of 44" fabric.)

3 Use scissors and a yardstick, or a rotary cutter and cutting mat, to cut the fabric.

Hem the edges

4 Make a 1" double-fold hem (see page 34) on both sides of each panel.

5 Hem the bottom edge with a double-fold hem that is pressed under ½", then 2½". Fold the corners at a slight angle so the ends won't poke out.

6 Finish the top edge according to the way you want to hang the curtains:
- ◆ If you want a casing for an inserted curtain rod, make a double-fold hem at the top edge wide enough to fit the rod with a couple of extra inches for a nice gather. For example, press under the top edge ½", then 4".

♦ If you're using curtain ring clips, the width of the hem is up to you. A 2" double-fold hem would be sufficient.

Hang the curtains

7   Insert the rod through the casing, or attach six curtain ring clips per curtain, evenly spaced. Hang the curtain.

8   If you like, use cording to tie back the curtains — high, low, or wherever you wish.

Ravioli Floor Pillow

Fabulous floor pillows can turn your tween's room into a truly hip hangout. Even older kids can't resist a comfy spot on the floor or a floppy pillow to prop themselves up in bed. We made ours reversible and used coordinating fabrics so they'll go with the rest of the room. Stitching the flange with the pillow inside is a little cumbersome, but it's so worth it to have the extra bit of flair along the edges.

Our finished size

31½" square (fits a 26" square pillow)

Reversible furnishings are super for kids and tweens whose moods and favorites can shift as quickly as you can flip a pillow!

What you'll need

- ◆ 26" square pillow form
- ◆ 1 yard of fabric per side

Measure and cut the fabric

1 Measure and cut two 32" square pieces of fabric.

Stitch the sides

2 Pin the two squares with right sides together. Stitch all around the outer edge, leaving a 10" to 12" opening at the center of one side; backstitch on both sides of the opening.

3 Trim the corners and turn the pillow cover right side out. Tuck in the seam allowances along the opening and press the pillow.

Make the flange

4 Topstitch all around the pillow, 2½" from the edge, leaving a 10" to 12" opening next to the other opening. We also stitched a diagonal line at each corner.

Insert the pillow form

5 Insert the pillow form through the openings. Slip-stitch the opening at the edge closed and complete topstitching flange opening. If you like, you could also edgestitch ¼" from the outside edge.

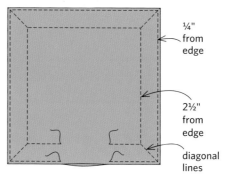

¼" from edge

2½" from edge

diagonal lines

EXTRA PIZZAZZ

For a little extra flair, we covered the lamp shade with fabric to match the Pom-Pom Pillow (see next page). The lamp shade cover is simple to make; just follow the general instructions for the Night-Light Lamp Shade Cover on page 115. Whether you re-cover the shade or not, you can add a strip of pom-poms to the bottom edge of any lamp shade with a hot glue gun.

Pom-Pom Pillow

The simplest pillow on the planet just got cool. And just you watch how quickly a sassy little pillow can help change a space! We went with pom-poms, but you can add fringe, tassels, beading, buttons, or piping. Embellish any way you want; these little decorative touches bring bits of personality to a room.

Our finished size

8" x 13"

What you'll need

- ⅔ yard of fabric
- 1½ yards of pom-pom fringe
- Polyester fiberfill stuffing

Measure and cut the fabric

1 Fold the fabric with right sides together. Near the selvage on the wrong side of the fabric, measure and draw a 9" x 14" rectangle. Cut two.

Add the pom-pom fringe

2 Lay one fabric rectangle on a flat surface, right side up. Pin the pom-pom fringe around the perimeter, lining up the edge of the pom-pom base with the raw edges (pom-poms lying on top of the fabric, not outside of it). Machine-baste ¼" from the edge.

Stitch the pillow

3 Lay the second fabric rectangle on top of the other, right sides together, and pin around the raw edges. Stitch on all sides, leaving a 5" to 7" opening; backstitch on both sides of the opening.

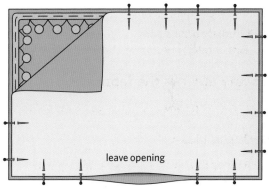

leave opening

STEPS 2 & 3

Turn and stuff

4 Clip the corners (see page 32) and turn the pillow right side out. Stuff with polyester fiberfill or other stuffing, and slipstich the opening closed.

Hanging Caddy

Hang this adorable caddy over a bedside table, desk, or on a door to give access to the essentials. It makes a great charging station, too. We made sure our pockets would fit a phone or music player, as well as some useful tools or a pocket dictionary. Map out what you'd like to fit in the pockets and tailor your design to suit the needs of your tween.

Our finished size
9" x 12½"

What you'll need
- ½ yard or 2 fat quarters of two contrasting fabrics
- 14" dowel
- 2 large hooks sized to fit the dowel

HANG-UPS

To hang the dowel, we used teacup hooks, available at any hardware store and some craft stores. For easy access, hang the caddy along the side of the bed. If the layout of the room doesn't work for that, and you decide to hang it at the head of the bed, just make sure to hang it high enough to avoid your tween hitting his or her head on the teacup hooks.

Measure and cut the fabric

1   Measure and cut two 15½" x 13½" rectangles. Or, if making a custom size, add 1" to the width of the desired finished size (for seam allowance) and add enough to the length to allow for the folded bottom and top casing (we added 6½").

VARIATION

It's all about the embellishments! Creatively trimmed pillows can add that much-needed zip of color to complete a look.

Make a channel for the dowel

4 Press under the top edge 1½" (toward the back fabric) and stitch in place, backstitching at both ends.

Stitch the pockets

5 With the front fabric facing up, fold up the bottom edge 4" and press. Pin the sides and mark where you want the pocket divisions to be. Stitch the sides, then stitch the pockets, backstitching each time at the top edge to reinforce.

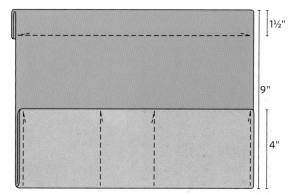

Hang the caddy

6 Drill holes and install two large hooks into the wall at the desired location, with the outer edges 14" apart. Insert the dowel through the channel on the caddy, with ends sticking out on each side. Hang the caddy by placing the dowel ends into the hooks.

Stitch the body

2 Pin the two fabrics together, right sides facing. Decide which will be the back fabric. If using directional fabric, keep in mind that the bottom 4" of the back fabric will be folded up to the front. That means it should be upside down in back, so it will be right side up when folded.

3 Stitch around all raw edges, leaving a 5" opening on the bottom edge for turning; backstitch on both sides of the opening. Clip the corners (see page 32) and turn right side out. Tuck in the seam allowance along the opening and press. Edgestitch along the bottom edge, closing the opening in the process.

One Space, Three Functions

Adding sewn accessories to a room can change not only the look of the space, but its function as well. Here we'll look at a simple table in a corner, and show how easily you can transform it to suit your needs. First up: A home office. Even a work space can have some style! The next option is a dressing table — an old-fashioned notion to some, perhaps, but an acceptable luxury in my book. Last but not least: the craft studio. A dedicated craft area may be an even bigger luxury than the dressing table, but you (and your art) are worth it!

Vanity Fair

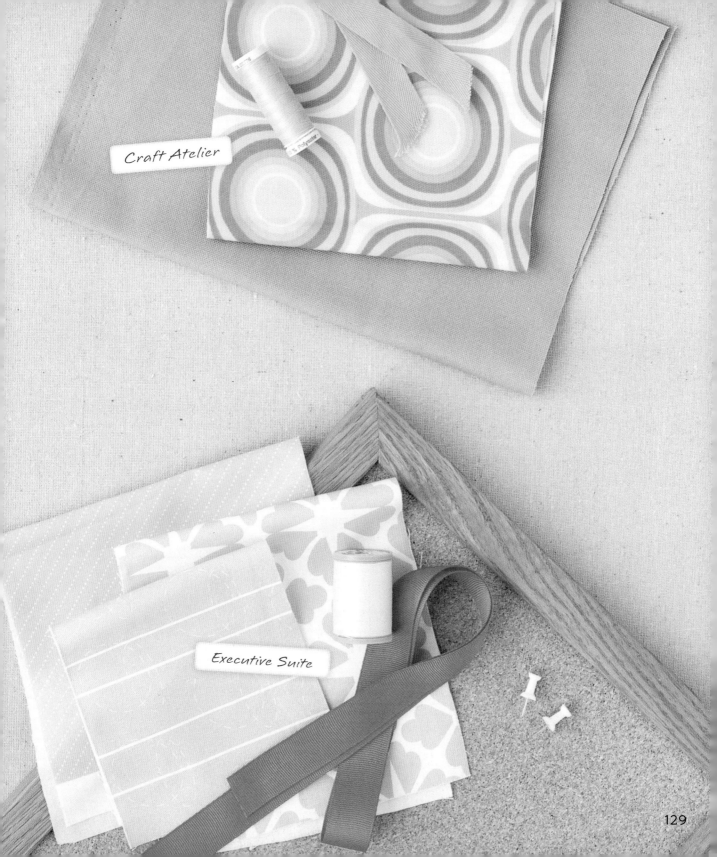

Craft Atelier

Executive Suite

129

CHAPTER 13

Executive Suite

WHEN YOU WORK FROM HOME, it's imperative to carve out a space for creativity and productivity that won't take over your entire house. Choose your station carefully, then do your best to contain your work within its perimeter. No matter how much space you have, your basic needs will be the same. You want to have the right tools for the job within reach so you can access them quickly when you need them — and keep them out of sight when you don't. By using coordinating fabrics and colors like we did, a boring little corner becomes a dashing, distinctive work space. The challenge in selecting fabric for a spot like this is to choose patterns that are fairly subtle and complementary in the same or pleasingly similar color shades, so they don't compete with the other elements on and around your desktop.

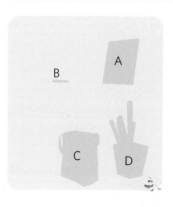

A. *Memo Board*

B. *Journal Cover*

C. *Mobile Office Tote*

D. *Fabric-Covered Wastebasket*

Memo Board

This simple, covered corkboard lets you see what's coming — and what you've accomplished. Hidden pockets at the bottom let you stash tickets for upcoming events, so you won't forget them, or pens and tools you want to keep handy. We chose a classic fabric reminiscent of kitchen tiles to keep the look fresh and crisp. Too much clutter can be distracting and the goal here is to stay organized and on top of your game!

Our finished size

17" square

What you'll need

- 1 framed corkboard
- ¾ yard of fabric, depending on the size of your board
- An additional ¼ yard of the same or coordinating fabric for the pocket panel
- Staple gun and staples

Measure and cut the fabric

1 On the wrong side of the fabric, mark a square the size of your corkboard plus 2" on all sides (ours was 21" square). Cut it out.

2 On the wrong side of the fabric, mark a rectangle for the pocket panel that is 6½" x the width of your corkboard.

Stitch the pocket panel

3 Stitch a ½" double-fold hem (see page 34) along the top edge of the pocket panel. Press under a ½" single-fold hem on the opposite (bottom) raw edge, but do not stitch.

4 Lay the large fabric square on a flat surface. Mark a point 2" up from the bottom edge on both the left and right side. Unfold the bottom edge of the pocket panel and line up the fold with the 2" marks. Stitch from one side to the other along the folded crease.

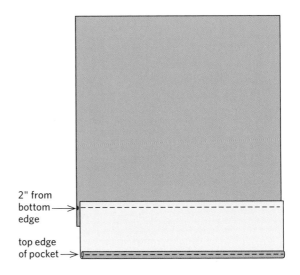

2" from bottom edge →

top edge of pocket →

5 Turn the pocket up against the fabric, where it will be on the board, and press along the stitching line.

6 Measure and mark the desired pocket widths and stitch the dividing lines, backstitching at both ends.

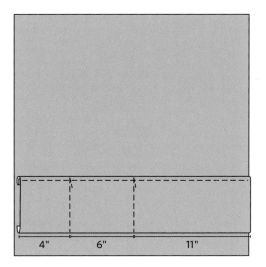

4" 6" 11"

Attach the fabric to the board

7 Lay the fabric on a flat surface, wrong side facing up. Center the corkboard on top of it. Pull the raw edges of the fabric over the bottom side of the board, aligning the bottom edge of the pocket with the frame edge, and staple it onto the frame. Do the same with the opposite/top edge, pulling the fabric tight and smoothing out any wrinkles.

8 Staple the left and right sides last, folding the fabric neatly at the corners.

Journal Cover

These days, we're more likely to post our feelings and thoughts somewhere on the Internet than we are to write them down in a journal. Call me old-fashioned, but I still carry a journal with me at all times because good ideas can strike at any time. Like writing by hand, making a cover for your journal can help you feel more connected to your own thoughts and enhance the journaling experience.

Our finished size

3⅞" x 5⅞" (journal closed)

What you'll need

- small journal
- ¼ yard of 2 fabrics or fabric scraps for cover and lining
- Additional fabric scraps for embellishment (we used chalkboard oilcloth)
- Spray adhesive (see Safety First! on page 28)

Measure your journal

1 Every journal is different, so you need to plot the size of yours. For the height, measure the closed journal, then add ¼" for ease and 1" for seam allowance. To find the width, you need to allow for flaps inside the journal. Take the following two measurements and add them together:

- With the journal closed, measure from the edge of the front cover, around the spine, to the edge of the back cover, then add 1¼".
- Open up the journal and measure the width of the inside front cover. Subtract 2" from that and multiply by two.

Measure and cut the fabric

2 Measure and mark rectangles on the wrong side of the exterior fabric and the lining. Cut them out.

Stitch the journal cover

3 With right sides facing, pin the lining and exterior fabrics together. Stitch around the outer edges, leaving an opening at one of the short ends (where the flaps will be) for turning.

4 Trim the corners and turn the fabrics right side out. Tuck the seam allowances neatly into the opening and press. Edgestitch ¼" from both side edges, closing the opening in the process.

5 With the right side up, fold over the stitched side flaps, following your measurement for the inside cover. Pin in place and edgestitch ¼" across the top and bottom of each flap to secure.

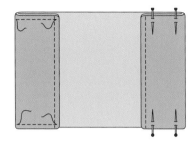

6 Turn the cover right side out and press, turning the top and bottom inner edges ¼" to the lining side.

Embellish

7 Add appliqués, embroidery stitches, or whatever strikes your fancy. We cut two small rectangles with pinking shears, the smallest one from chalkboard oilcloth, and attached them, one on top of the other, with a spray adhesive. A chalk pencil can then be used to label the journal.

VARIATIONS

Give each one of your journals a different look depending on its function.

Mobile Office Tote

A "mobile office" tote can keep clutter at bay by helping you sort your projects or tasks into different totes. Attach a label to the handles or assign a different color or pattern to each project. For those of us who like to "travel" from one spot to another in the home (kitchen table, anyone?), having a mobile office tote can be a lifesaver.

Our finished size

14" wide x 14½" tall (not including handles)

What you'll need

- ⅔ yard of sturdy fabric (see A Sense of Direction below)
- 2¾ yards of 1" cotton webbing (see Short Stack next page)

A SENSE OF DIRECTION

Since you are only using one piece of fabric to make this tote, you'll need to choose your fabric carefully. If your fabric has a directional print, one side will have the design going the wrong way. If you want to use a directional print, you'll need to cut the body panel into two pieces, turn one piece in the opposite direction, and stitch them together before making your tote.

Measure and cut

1 Measure and mark a 21" x 38" rectangle on the wrong side of the fabric.

Hem the top edges

2 The short ends of the rectangle will become the top edges of the bag. Press both under ½", then another 1". Pin and stitch.

Make and attach the straps

3 Fold your bag fabric in thirds lengthwise, making two light creases for handle placement. Open the fabric back up and lay it flat. Pin webbing handles along the creases as shown so the ends of the strap overlap slightly in the middle (the joint will end up on the bottom of the bag). Tuck under the end of the top strap. Stitch the strap in place.

4 Add a box stitch at the top of each strip (see page 31).

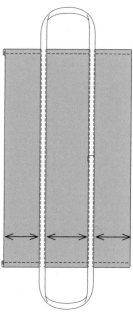

bag divided in thirds across the bottom

Stitch the sides

5 With right sides together, fold the fabric panel with the straps at the top and pin along the raw edges. Stitch the sides using a zigzag stitch. Press seam allowances to one side.

Make the gussets

6 With the tote still inside out, pull out the fabric on both sides of a side seam to form a triangle at the bottom. Measure 3½" from the point and draw a straight line across the corner with fabric pencil or chalk. Stitch along the line, using a zigzag stitch. Do the same on the remaining corner.

7 Turn the tote right side out, flattening the stitched triangles into the bottom of the bag. If desired, stitch neatly along each side seam to reinforce.

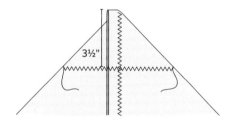

SHORT STACK

You can make a handheld tote with short handles or try longer straps to sling over your shoulder. Play with different lengths to find your favorites. Just for fun, we used the same fabric but turned the stripes in a different direction. For a sturdier tote, fuse extra-stiff interfacing to the fabric before stitching it up.

Fabric-Covered Wastebasket

There's nothing sexy about a garbage can . . . or is there? Dressing up your mess is probably one of the best things you can do for your "circular file." Since we all need a wastebasket, why settle for something dull or ugly? Why not go that extra mile? This is a no-sew, easy project that (most definitely) brightens up the nasty chore of taking out the trash.

Our finished size

10" tall with 8½" sides (at the top)

What you'll need

- A wooden or plastic wastebasket (see Project Notes below)
- Heavyweight paper for a template
- ½ yard of fabric, depending on the size of your can
- Spray adhesive (see Safety First! on page 28)
- 1 yard of ¼" ribbon

PROJECT NOTES

Our wastebasket has nice, flat sides, but if yours is a cylinder, it's just as easy. Just measure and cut a rectangle to fit around the circumference and stick in place. The ribbon on the top edge will hide any imperfections and presto! Your trash has class!

Make a template

1 On a flat surface, trace one side of your wastebasket onto heavyweight paper. Add ½" to both sides and bottom, but not at the top. Cut out the template.

Cut the fabric

2 Trace the template onto the wrong side of the fabric and cut out four panels.

Attach the fabric

3 With the wastebasket on its side, check the fit by placing a fabric panel on one side panel. Line up the top edge and let ½" hang over the remaining edges. Adjust as needed. Then lay the fabric flat on a protected surface, wrong side facing up, and apply spray adhesive, following manufacturer's instructions. Press the fabric onto the side of the wastebasket to secure, pressing the ½" margins past the edges to the other sides.

4 Turn the wastebasket so the opposite side is facing up and repeat step 3.

5 For the remaining panels, working one at a time, press under the sides ½", then place on the wastebasket to make sure the pressed edges are flush with the side edges. When you are happy with the alignment, apply the spray adhesive and affix those pieces of fabric.

Add the trim

6 Attach the ribbon with spray adhesive, turning one end under to overlap the other end and trimming away excess.

VARIATIONS

Once you start looking around your office with a creative eye, nearly every surface presents an opportunity to showcase fabric. A plain metal file tray is dressed up with a fabric covering with elasticized edging. An eyeglass case and cup cover offer open invitations.

CHAPTER 14

Vanity Fair

TAKING CARE OF YOURSELF AND YOUR TINY TREASURES IS IMPORTANT.
Designating a special spot for pampering yourself is the best way to
ensure you'll do it. It's not always easy to find time, but it's important
to treat yourself to a little TLC. You deserve a makeover from time to
time, too! The soft touch of fabric is perfect for holding jewelry and
other valuables. The pieces we designed for this table can be easily
modified or personalized to fit your particular tastes and needs. Look
for fabric that color-coordinates with your bedroom or bath and make
up additional fabric trays to jazz up your dresser top or bathroom
vanity. And what a great gift these items make for a friend who could
use a little TLC, as well.

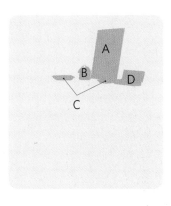

A. *Jewelry Display*

B. *Wristlet Pouch*

C. *Pinwheel Tray*

D. *"My Precious" Ring Box*

Jewelry Display

Hang up your earrings and bangles and keep track of necklaces once and for all. Basically, all you need is a framed corkboard, fabric, and some ribbon, twill tape, or cording. We hung our display vertically so we'd have room for a mirror — well, it's called a "vanity" for a reason, right? — but of course you can go horizontal if you feel like it. Just measure and cut accordingly.

Our finished size

18" x 22"

What you'll need

- Framed corkboard
- Fabric, enough to cover the board
- Spray adhesive (see Safety First! on page 28)
- 4 yards of ¼" twill tape
- 20 or more thumbtacks
- 5 cup hooks

Measure and cut the fabric

1 Measure the height and width of your corkboard from inside the edges of the frame. Cut one piece of fabric to those exact measurements.

Affix the fabric

2 Apply spray adhesive to the wrong side of the fabric, following manufacturer's instructions. Flip the fabric over and fit it into the frame, smoothing over the corkboard as you go and pressing firmly into place.

Attach the twill tape

3 Move the strips of twill tape around until you're satisfied with the layout. We placed ours 2" from the top edge, then added another strip every 3¼". Secure both ends of each strip with a tack, then insert three more tacks across the tape, evenly spaced.

Attach cup hooks

4 Insert the cup hooks just below the top of the frame by twisting them into the cork with the hooks pointing up.

You can pick up 12" cork squares and a frame in most craft stores. Just affix a square of fabric to the cork and pop it into the frame. If the frame is deeper than your cork square, hot-glue two squares together before adding the fabric.

Wristlet Pouch

This adorable pouch can be perched at home on your vanity table, stuffed with makeup brushes and your special little tools. Or you can wear it out on the town, with your on-the-go beauty kit stashed inside. See, you can take it with you!

Our finished size

5" across the bottom x 6½" high, not including strap

What you'll need

- ¼ yard of fabric
- 6" piece of double-sided fusible interfacing
- ⅓ yard of ¼" elastic

Measure and cut

1 Mark, measure, and cut the following pieces:
   - Two 6" circles from fabric, plus one from interfacing
   - 7¾" x 18" fabric rectangle for the body
   - 2" x 14" fabric strip for the strap

Fuse the interfacing

2 Lay the two circles together with wrong sides facing, then slip the interfacing between the two fabrics. Press to fuse together.

Make a casing

3 On the top (long) edge of the rectangle, press under ¼", then another ½". Pin and edgestitch the double-folded edge to create a casing.

Assemble the pouch

4 Staystitch ½" from the bottom of the edge of the rectangle, all the way across. Clip every inch or so along the bottom edge, taking care not to cut through the staystitching.

5 With right sides together, pin the bottom of the rectangle to the fused circles, spreading the clips and easing the fabric around the circle. We've left the sides open to allow some room for adjustment.

6 With right sides together, stitch up the side of the bag, stopping at the top just below the casing, and backstitch. Trim excess seam allowance and press seams open.

Thread the elastic

7 Use a safety pin to pull the elastic through one end of the casing and out the other. Pull the elastic and adjust for the amount of gathering you like, then overlap the ends of the elastic and secure with a zigzag stitch. Hand-sew the opening to close the casing.

Make and attach the strap

8 Make a strap from the 14" strip, as if making bias tape (see page 34), by pressing the fabric strip in half lengthwise, and pressing under ¼" on both sides. Stitch along the edge.

9 With the pouch inside out, pin the ends of the strap to opposite sides, on the inside of the bag. Stitch the ends ¼" from the top edge of the pouch, then stitch again below the first stitch line to secure the strap. Do the same on the other side, then turn the bag right side out.

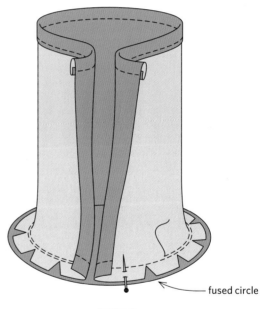

fused circle

STEP 5

Pinwheel Tray

Makeup, jewelry, watches, cell phone — give them a spot to call home. These little trays can be whipped up really fast, so you can make a bunch. They're perfect for the dressing table. You can make them any size, they don't break if you knock one over while blow-drying your hair, and they hold just about anything to help keep you organized — and your vanity looking fabulous, dahling.

Our finished sizes

4" square and 7" square

What you'll need

- ◆ 2 complementary fabrics (see step 1)
- ◆ Fusible interfacing

Measure and cut the fabric

1 For each tray you want to make, decide how large you want the finished tray to be (across the bottom), then add 4" for the sides and 1" for seam allowance. Cut two squares, one from each fabric, and also cut a piece of fusible interfacing the same size.

Assemble the tray pieces

2 Decide which will be the top fabric, and fuse the interfacing to the wrong side.

3 Pin the fabrics together with right sides facing. Stitch around the edges, leaving a 2" to 3" opening. Trim corners and trim any excess seam allowances, except for the edges along the opening.

4 Turn the fabrics right side out, tuck in the seam allowance along the opening, and press. Edge-stitch all the way around the square, closing the opening as you go. Add a second row of stitches ¼" from the first, if desired.

Stitch the corners

5 Fold the tray into a triangle and press the corners. Mark and stitch each corner, backstitching at the ends. Fold the tray in the opposite direction and repeat on the remaining two corners. Open the tray and press the side edges to make a crease.

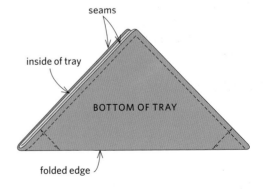

seams

inside of tray

BOTTOM OF TRAY

folded edge

STEP 5

VARIATIONS

Once you master this simple pattern, you can customize the sizes to fit your needs.

"My Precious" Ring Box

Stop searching for your favorite baubles at the back of the drawer and slip those babies into this cozy box, just right for even the most precious rings. Be sure to measure your rings, especially if you've got large or unusually shaped ones. You can always make the buttonholes a tiny bit too big, but cut the slits in the foam smaller, so the rings will fit just right.

Our finished insert size

3" x 10¼"

What you'll need

- ◆ 1 box with a hinged lid
- ◆ 1 piece of 1"–1½" foam, large enough to fit the box
- ◆ Fabric scrap to fit the inside of the box
- ◆ Single-sided, fusible, medium-weight interfacing
- ◆ Mat knife
- ◆ Spray adhesive (see Safety First! on page 28)

Measure, cut, and fuse

1 Measure the inside dimensions of the box, and cut a piece of foam to fit snugly inside it. (We had to glue two pieces together to get the right height.)

2 Cut one piece of fabric and one piece of interfacing the same size.

3 Fuse the interfacing to the wrong side of the fabric.

Make buttonholes

4 Move your rings around to find the best arrangement, and then mark the desired buttonhole locations on the interfaced side of the fabric. If you want straight rows, like ours, use a ruler to measure and trace lines across the length of the box.

5 You can machine-stitch using a buttonhole attachment, or you can "fake it" like we did by stitching two rows of tight zigzag stitches and joining the ends with a satin stitch. When finished, carefully cut open each buttonhole.

Cut slits in the foam

6 Place the fabric on top of the foam and mark the ring slots by poking a pencil through each buttonhole and drawing a line. Remove the fabric and check the markings by holding up some of your rings to be sure the lines aren't too wide. If they look good, use a mat or utility knife to cut slits along the lines, cutting only as deep as you need to for the rings to fit, generally about ½". You might want to test this out on a piece of scrap foam before making the cuts.

Affix fabric to foam

7 Apply spray adhesive to the wrong side of the fabric, following manufacturer's instructions; also spray the top of the foam and wait about 10 seconds so both surfaces are tacky. With right side up, place the fabric onto the foam, lining up the buttonholes with the slots beneath. Smooth and finger-press once everything is aligned.

NOTE: *Before the adhesive dries, be sure to gently run your mat knife through the slots to make sure they aren't sticking closed.*

FINAL TOUCH
If you like, paint the box a color that will complement the fabric interior.

CHAPTER 15

Craft Atelier

NOW THAT YOU'VE COME TO THE LAST SECTION OF THE BOOK, you might be thinking you need a dedicated craft space, if you don't have one already! Again, with just a table and a single chair, we not only created space for doing the work and some storage to boot, we also found clever ways to organize and increase efficiency. By the way, the solid fabric we use in these projects is canvas, which we recommend for strength and durability. The blue-and-white fabric is laminated cotton, which makes a sturdy, waterproof, wipeable surface. You could also use oilcloth, or just plain canvas for all the fabrics, if you don't care about waterproofing.

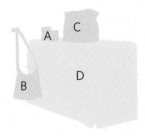

A. *Canvas Coffee Cans*

B. *Artist's Sling*

C. *Sewing Machine Cover*

D. *Utilitarian Table Cover*

Canvas Coffee Cans

In art school, you get a rusty coffee can for your brushes and tools. In your own atelier, however, you can step it up a notch or two with some fabulously functional canvas "cans." These sturdy containers stand up on their own and make your worktable look very professional and polished. The top can be folded to either side, making the can reversible.

Our finished size

5" across x 7" high (unfolded)

What you'll need

- ¼ yard of solid canvas
- ¼ yard of printed canvas

Measure and cut

1 Measure and cut two 6" circles; these could both be from one fabric, or one from each.

2 Measure and cut one 8" x 18" rectangle from each fabric.

Stitch exterior and lining

3 Staystitch ½" from the bottom of each rectangle edge, all the way across. Clip every inch or so along the bottom edge, taking care not to cut through the staystitching.

4 With right sides together, pin and stitch the bottom of one rectangle to a circle, spreading the clips and easing the fabric around the circle. We've left the sides open to allow some room for adjustment. Attach the remaining rectangle to the remaining circle in the same way.

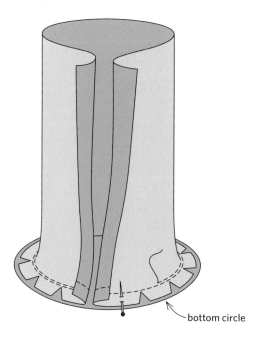

bottom circle

For a change of look, turn it inside out!

5 Stitch up the side of each cylinder, trim off excess seam allowance, and press seams open.

Assemble and stitch

6 Turn the exterior solid canvas right side out. With wrong sides together, slip the printed canvas into the exterior. By hand, turn under both fabrics ½" to the inside, so the raw edges are hidden between the fabrics. Pin, then edgestitch to join the inner and outer fabrics.

7 Fold the top edge down 2" to 3" to show the print inside.

Artist's Sling

Inspired by scissor bags, used by fast-moving uber-stylists in the finest salons, this sling is designed to offer easy access to your most frequently used tools. It might be pens or brushes, maybe a tape measure and tailor's chalk — or cutting tools, pliers, and so on. Use this project as a guideline to fashion your own sling, and tweak the pockets to hold exactly what you need. (By the way, this makes a great cash bag for craft fairs!)

Our finished size
10" x 10½"

What you'll need
- ½ yard of solid canvas
- Canvas scraps for pockets

Measure and cut the fabric

1 Measure and cut the following pieces:

- Two 10½" x 11¾" rectangles
- 2 pocket panels as shown (we used laminated cotton for these)
- 3" x 54" strap (if you are using 54"-wide canvas, you can cut one long strip along the width; otherwise, cut two 28" strips and stitch the ends together)

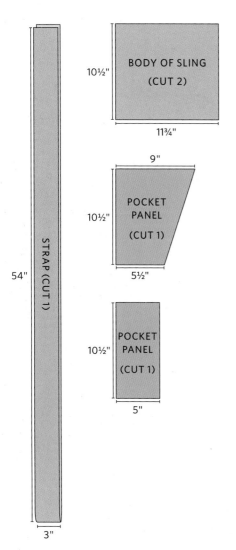

STRAP (CUT 1)

54"

3"

BODY OF SLING
(CUT 2)

10½"

11¾"

9"

POCKET
PANEL
(CUT 1)

10½"

5½"

POCKET
PANEL
(CUT 1)

10½"

5"

Make the strap

2 Make the strap as you would double-fold bias tape (see page 34), by pressing the fabric strip in half lengthwise and pressing under ½" on both sides. Edgestitch the strap.

Hem the pieces

3 Make a ½" double-fold hem on the top of both body panels.

4 If using laminated cotton, you only need a ½" single-fold hem on the top edge of each pocket panel. Otherwise, make a ¼" double-fold hem.

Stitch on the pockets

5 Lay the front body panel on a flat surface, right side up. Pin the taller pocket panel to the body panel, right side up, aligning the bottom edges and sides. Pin the shorter pocket on over the tall pocket in the same way.

6 Draw a vertical line down the center of the pockets, or wherever you want the pocket divisions to be. Stitch along the line, backstitching at the top hemmed edge to reinforce.

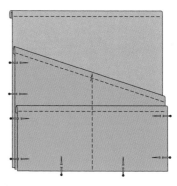

Stitch the sides and straps

7 With right sides together, pin the back body panel over the front. Insert the strap ends at a slight angle between the body panels, just below the

stitched top edge, as shown. Then trim the strap ends. Stitch all around sides and bottom, using a zigzag stitch. Finish the seam allowance with a zigzag stitch, if desired, trim the lower corners, and turn right side out.

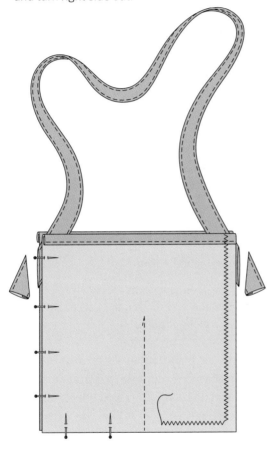

CUSTOMIZED POCKETS

If your favorite hobby is knitting or crochet, add additional stitching lines to step 6 to create a series of tighter-fitting pockets for holding knitting needles or crochet hooks securely. You could also stitch pocket lines just along the taller pocket panel (step 5) to hold pencils, brushes, or other small accessories. It's your bag — make it fit your needs!

Sewing Machine Cover

Even if you sew a lot, it's still a good idea to cover your sewing machine when it's not being used. It will keep your machine from getting dusty, which will help it last longer — and it looks great, too! We made ours with two different fabrics: one with a print and one just a simple solid. If you are using a directional fabric, don't forget to put this together with the fabric going the right way.

Our finished size
12½" x 19"

What you'll need
♦ ½ yard of two fabrics, or 1 yard if using only one fabric

Measure and cut

1 Measure your sewing machine from the top center to the tabletop. Be sure to allow for half the depth of the machine. Add 2" to this measurement. Measure from side to side in the same way, adding half the depth of the machine, and add 1". These are the two dimensions you will need to cut the fabric.

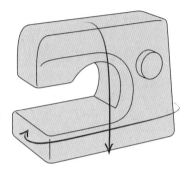

2 On the wrong side of each fabric, use your dimensions to draw a rectangle. Cut out two pieces, one front and one back.

Stitch the pieces

3 Make a ½" double-fold hem (see page 34) on the bottom edge of each rectangle.

4 With right sides together, pin the two rectangles, matching up all raw edges. Stitch up one side, across the top, and down the other side, backstitching at both ends.

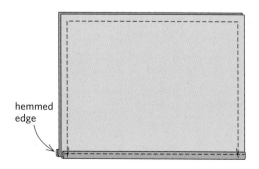

hemmed edge

Make the top corner gussets

5 With the cover still inside out, pull out the fabric on both sides of a seamed corner to form a triangle at the bottom. On both sides of the corner, measure 3" to 3½" from the point and draw a straight line across the corner with fabric pencil or chalk. Stitch along the line, then trim off the corner with pinking shears. Do the same on the remaining corner. Turn right side out and place over the sewing machine.

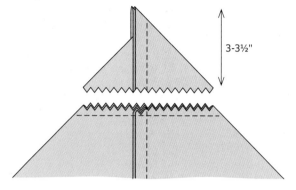

3-3½"

Utilitarian Table Cover

When you're working on your craft, you want all of your tools and supplies at your fingertips. Keeping an orderly and accessible workstation offers the most room for inspiration and creativity. This table cover is practical and attractive, and can easily transform any table into your very own studio. We made it floor length on all four sides with tie closures at the corners, so we could easily stow more stuff underneath and access it easily.

Our finished size

20" x 48"; sides are 28"

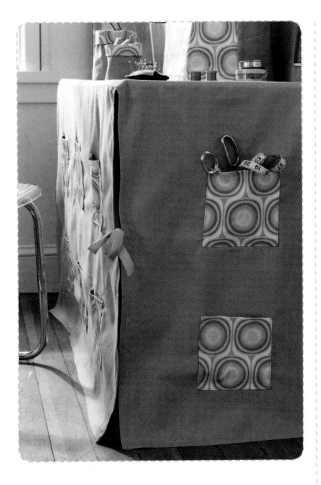

Measure and cut the pieces

1   Following the diagram, measure the top of your table for width and add 1" for seam allowances. The length will be the top of the table plus the height on the side ends, plus 2" for hems. Cut one long piece from the canvas that will go up one end of the table, across the top, and down the other end. Measure and mark the four corners of the table top, so you'll know where to attach the front and back side panels.

2   For the front and back side panels, measure the front of the table: the length across the top X the height of the table. Add 2" to the length for hems, and 1¾" to the height for seam allowance plus hem. Cut two pieces from canvas.

What you'll need

♦ 3 yards of 54"-wide canvas, depending on the size of your table
♦ ½ yard of canvas fabric for the pockets
♦ 3⅓ yards of ¾" twill tape for the ties

FABRIC NOTE

If you're working with laminated canvas, remember that the vinyl isn't forgiving like cotton or other woven materials. If you mess up your stitches, the holes will show. Sew up your pockets carefully or switch to canvas instead.

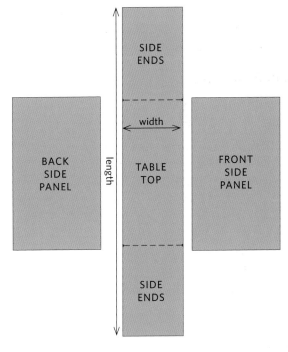

STEPS 1 & 2

3 From the pocket fabric, cut eight 7" square pieces (or cut the size you prefer, adding 1" to height and width for seam allowance).

4 For the ties, cut eight strips of twill tape approximately 15" long.

Stitch and attach the pockets

5 Make a ¼" double-fold hem on the top edge of each pocket. With wrong side up, press under the remaining sides ½" and pin.

6 Lay the pockets on the front side panel as you like (we put six pockets on the front, about 6" from the top and 8" apart; and two pockets on one side end). Measure from the top of the fabric to both top corners of each pocket, to make sure they are straight, then pin each pocket in place.

7 Stitch each pocket, starting on one side with a backstitch, then stitch around the bottom and up the other side, finishing with a backstitch.

Attach the sides

8 Make a ½" double-fold hem (see page 34) on the bottom edge of the front side panel, then do the same on the sides. Leave the top edge raw. Repeat for the back side panel. Press.

9 With right sides together, pin the front side to the top, aligning raw edges and positioning the panels between the marks you made in step 1. Stitch in place, backstitching at both ends. Stitch the back panel to the top in the same way.

10 Turn both side pieces outward (making a large cross) and press the seams toward the center piece. Also press under the side edges of the top ½". Stitch the side edges to make a single-fold hem (or, if you prefer, a ¼" double-fold hem).

11 Make a ½" double-fold hem on the bottom raw edge of both side ends. Press.

Attach the ties

12 With the wrong side out, position the cover on the table it was made to fit. Measure about 11" from each top corner and mark where the ties will be. Fold under one end of each strip of twill tape and pin it to the seam allowance as shown. Stitch all eight strips in place. Cut the raw end on the diagonal.

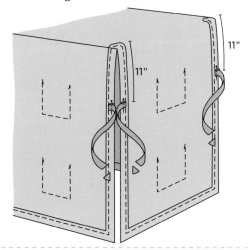

HIT THE ROAD, JACK!

This table cover isn't just perfect for your studio or creative space at home, it's also the perfect customized table cover for taking on the road to craft fairs! Just turn it around so the pockets are in the back, and you can stash all kinds of supplies back there. You have the option of decorating the unpocketed side with your logo or name, so it becomes your storefront when you flip it around. Make your display eye-catching and watch customers flock your way!

NOTE: We made this table cover to fit a simple folding table at home. If you want to take one to shows, be sure to find out the size of the table you'll be getting and make a cover that fits those dimensions. If you keep a similarly sized table at home, you can practice laying out your display so you're really ready come show time!

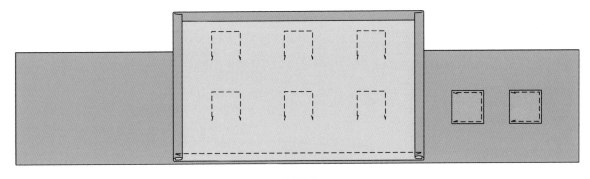

STEP 9

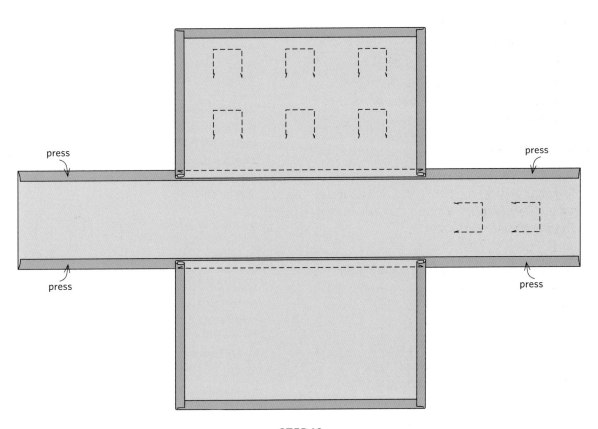

press

press

press

press

STEP 10

Resources

Sewing Machine Information

Sew USA
www.sewusa.com

Sewing & Craft Alliance
www.sewing.org

Sewing at About
http://sewing.about.com

Singer Sewing Co.
www.singerco.com

Tias.com
www.tias.com

Fabrics & Notions

The best way to select fabric is hands-on. Check your local phone book under "fabric shops" or "quilting" for local sources of fabrics, tools, and notions. You can also find all kinds of sewing supplies, tips, and ideas online at sites like these:

Annie Selke
www.annieselke.com

Bolt Fabric Boutique
www.boltfabricboutique.com

Cia's Palette
www.ciaspalette.com

Clotilde
www.clotilde.com

Crafty Planet
www.craftyplanet.com

Craigslist
www.craigslist.org

Denver Fabrics
www.denverfabrics.com

eBay
www.ebay.com

essentials
www.shopessentials.net

Etsy
www.etsy.com

The Freecycle Network
www.freecycle.org

Glorious Color
www.gloriouscolor.com

Harts Fabric
www.hartsfabric.com

Hawthorne Threads
www.hawthornethreads.com

jcaroline companies
www.jcarolinecreative.com
www.jcarolinehome.com

J&O Fabrics
www.jandofabrics.com

Jo-Ann Fabric & Craft Stores
www.joann.com

M&J Trimming
www.mjtrim.com

Maine Cottage
www.mainecottage.com

Mood Fabrics
www.moodfabrics.com

Peter Fasano
www.peterfasano.com

Purl Soho
www.purlsoho.com

SewZanne's Fabrics
www.sewzannesfabrics.com

Spoonflower
www.spoonflower.com

Sublime Stitching
www.sublimestitching.com

True Up (a blog devoted to fabric)
www.trueup.net

Waverly
www.waverly.com

Z&S Fabrics
www.zandsfabrics.com

Zarin Fabrics
www.zarinfabrics.com

Periodicals

Sew News
www.sewnews.com

Sewing Savvy Newsletter (Clotilde)
www.clotilde.com/sewing_savvy.php

Threads (Taunton Press)
www.threadsmagazine.com

Index

Other Storey Titles You Will Enjoy

One-Yard Wonders, by Rebecca Yaker and Patricia Hoskins.
101 hip, contemporary projects, from baby items and plush toys to pet
beds and stylish bags, each made from just a single yard of fabric.
304 pages. Hardcover with concealed wire-o and pattern insert. ISBN 978-1-60342-449-3.

The Quilting Answer Book, by Barbara Weiland Talbert.
Hundreds of solutions for every quilting quandary, guiding readers
through cutting, piecing, appliqué work, borders, and binding.
432 pages. Flexibind. ISBN 978-1-60342-144-7.

Sew & Stow, by Betty Oppenheimer.
Out with plastic bags and in with 30 practical and stylish totes of all types!
192 pages. Paper. ISBN 978-1-60342-027-3.

Sew What! Bags, by Lexie Barnes.
Totes, messenger bags, drawstring sacks, and handbags — 18 pattern-
free projects that can be customized into all shapes and sizes.
152 pages. Hardcover with concealed wire-o. ISBN 978-1-60342-092-1.

Sew What! Skirts, by Francesca DenHartog & Carole Ann Camp.
A fast, straightforward method of sewing a variety of inspired skirts that
fit your body perfectly, without relying on store-bought patterns.
128 pages. Hardcover with concealed wire-o. ISBN 978-1-58017-625-5.

The Sewing Answer Book, by Barbara Weiland Talbert.
A friendly, reassuring resource that answers beginning
and advanced sewing questions.
432 pages. Flexibind. ISBN 978-1-60342-543-8.

These and other books from Storey Publishing are available
wherever quality books are sold or by calling 1-800-441-5700.
Visit us at _www.storey.com._

3190105091 4219